Christian DNA Groups

A workbook for the first year

Nigel Coles

Published for Nigel Coles by Verité CM Ltd.

ISBN No: 978-1-907636-54-7

Print and production management by
Verité CM Ltd, Worthing,
West Sussex BN12 4HJ. UK.
www.veritecm.com

Dedication:

For my children,
Tom, Ben and Emily
and their generation.

Thanks:

Many thanks to Ruth Whiter for her design,
to Emily for her photograph on the cover
and Rachel for proof-reading.
To Maggie for her encouragement and patience

Do you want to be part of the adventure?

If you've bought a copy of Christian DNA groups, you have already taken a significant step towards exploring the adventure of God in your life. However, you also take the opportunity to contribute to the on-going development of deepening and spreading Christian DNA across the UK.

Whilst these materials have been tried and tested, I have no doubt they can be improved and developed, in order to be a greater encouragement for everyone getting involved.

I have committed myself to re-writing the basic material, on the basis of the first 1000 people working through it, for a year. You don't have to wait to feedback – this can be done, whenever you choose, via www.missionaldna.org

I shall also welcome any suggestions towards the development of other materials designed to deepen Christian DNA. You will soon realise, if you thought this was simply a reading book, you'll gain little, but if it's taken up and lived, you'll have something to say, so let's do this together.

FOLLOWING

…. from stagnation to momentum.

'Come follow me.' Jesus. [i]

'I have access to the work of Christ, only if I know the person who does this work.' Dietrich Bonhoeffer. [ii]

'Come follow me' – among the very first words of Jesus in Mark's gospel. On one level, they are simple to understand. The difficulty arises, as so often with Jesus' words, not because they are too difficult to understand, but because we understand them all too well! We then construct reasons to avoid their demands. There is no facet of life and no place in our hearts where we can avoid the challenge to apply these few simple, straightforward words. They are all embracing. These words go as deep as it gets. 'Come, follow me', just three words: simple yes, but all embracing. Bill Shankly, speaking of football, coined the phrase 'pass and move' as if it was 'all' football was about. "Keep it simple' was his motto, but easy? Hardly. Christian living, however, is no mere game.

Too often we view those who earn their income from the Church as the only ones who are 'called'. Think about how this perspective separates what Jesus intends for every disciple:

- We are *all* called by name.
- We are *all* called to live for him wherever we are.
- We are *all* called to offer all we are.

However long we live, we shall never get beyond the reach of these three words. The call to follow Jesus will always remain as the primary call upon us – whatever we might be called to do, or wherever we are called to go. In fact, before we *do* anything in the name of Jesus we must first hear these words. "Come follow me'.

Listening precedes following and doing, but without following it is highly questionable whether we have actually heard anything. Deitrich Bonhoeffer, said 'a Christianity without discipleship is a Christianity without Christ'.[iii] Jesus combines these two thoughts when he says 'whoever has my commands and keeps them is the one who loves me'. [iv] Every Christian quickly believes the truth of Jesus' words. Living them out is our difficulty. Is there an aspect of our life we need to give particular attention to for Jesus to be 'Lord of all'?

Do not separate what God has joined together. In this case, I'm talking about 'being' and 'doing'. In the Hebrew mind 'to know' something was only really true when that 'knowing' had been translated into practice. So, when the Bible speaks of a man 'knowing' a woman it is synonymous with having sex. In the New Testament, it explains why John writes 'we have come to know him if we keep his commands' [v]

One of our difficulties, in the western church, is the way we so often use the Bible. Consequently, we often think we've done something when actually all we've done is discuss it! Think about small group and individual discussions you've had recently – how many times do you find yourself thinking, 'that's interesting', or 'I don't agree with them', but have missed the point and done nothing. I'm a Baptist Minister and I often fall into the trap of talking about books, authors, ideas and theories as if I've tried and tested them all and found them wanting. Some Ministers don't even go as far as reading the book, just having it on their shelves is enough to convince them they've paid enough attention to its challenge. I often need to hear the words of DL Moody who responded, to those who criticised his methods of evangelism, with the words 'I prefer the way I do it to the way they don't.' [vi] It's an easy trap to fall into, but it remains a dangerous one. If only my prayer life reflected a little more the number of books I've read about it!

'What would Jesus do?' needs to become the watchword of every generation and not simply relegated to the wristbands worn by young people. 'Just do it' is the slogan made famous by Nike. Apparently, one day, after spending hours trying to find the right words to express their next big advertising campaign, someone, frustrated with the whole process, gave up and shouted 'just do it"! I wonder how frustrated Jesus might sometimes feel about the length of time we spend discussing the Bible and then going out and ignoring what we've shared because we've equated talking about something as doing it. As Michael Frost and Alan Hirsch have put it: 'the founder must be able to be seen in the lives of the found'. [vii]

One of the fundamental reasons why I advocate DNA groups meeting around the words of Jesus, for at least the first year, is because our greatest need, as the people of God in the United Kingdom, is to be re-rooted in the life of Jesus. It may well be you wish to focus upon another practice, which will help develop the habit of following Jesus, but none of us will get far if we neglect the basic spiritual discipline of listening to God. Our journey of following Jesus began when we stopped long enough to genuinely listen to the voice of God. Jesus called 'Simon, Andrew, James, John, Matthew, Philip, follow me'. Before anything else happened from a human perspective, they had to listen. Only having listened could they decide how they might respond. Practically, it is no different for us on a daily basis.

The comparison between the Sea of Galilee and the Dead Sea is often drawn upon by preachers, because there is such a dramatic distinction between the two. On the one hand, the Sea of Galilee is teeming with life – 24 species of fish apparently live there, the vegetation is lush and many animals make their nests in and around the surrounding banks. On the other hand, the Dead Sea did not gain its name for no reason. At 1400 feet below sea level, its shores are the lowest dry land on earth. Depending upon the season the water of the Dead sea is 35% salt. It's great for those photos of being able to float so easily, but hopeless in terms of supporting life. Apparently, microscopic bacteria live in it, but no fish, no animals and no plant material – it's dead! Now here's the really interesting bit – both bodies of water are fed by the Jordan River. However, whilst the Jordan continues from the Sea of Galilee into the Dead Sea there it comes to an end. Water flows into the Dead Sea, but does not flow out. It is so far below sea level, it has no outlet streams and loses 7 million tons of water daily by evaporation!

Our walk of discipleship will become static, or stagnant, if we attempt to live within a vacuum. The inter-relatedness of our relationships with God (D), one another (N) and ourselves (A) are not merely neat categories to think about, but the environment for living out our life in God. Any image involving the idea of following will concern momentum and our life of discipleship finds its momentum in both the overflow of our heart towards others and the in-flow from God's heart to ours. So where's the weakest link for you today?

Do I listen sufficiently to know what God is speaking into my life? Do I listen carefully enough to express his life in mine? How on earth do we practice listening to God?

Do I need to improve the environment in which I listen? For example, I used to 'feel' God only spoke to people whilst they're on holiday, but I now have come realise he's speaking all through the year – it's merely when we're away from the normal routines we often stop still long enough to hear what he's been saying all along.

Remember God has probably already spoken most of what we need to hear! There is often a danger we think listening to God is about hearing something new, whereas listening is essentially about hearing what has been spoken (primarily in the Bible). Do we need to take our personal reading of the Bible more slowly, read more regularly, read less more deeply, or allow more time in prayer during which we're not speaking to him!

Recognise we can all learn to listen more carefully.
Think about specific times when you believe God has spoken certain things to you. What is it, which you feel has brought the sense of certainty it was God? Can this process help you cultivate a keener listening ear?

Reflect on the fact God may communicate to us through a variety of different means - the bible, visions, dreams, nature, imagination, spiritual gifts given to ourselves or others, etc. It is worth asking yourself how you check out it is God's voice you're hearing. Dare you submit what you think you're hearing to others?

Do I need to tune in to God? Space, time, busyness, denial, sin, unwillingness to hear, my need to change. There are many things, which could be the reason why we don't make time to listen to God. You may wish to use your DNA group as a sounding board and listen to what they say! Different people find different things helpful – a long solitary walk, talking things through, or a retreat. The point is, find what helps you and make sure there's space for it.

Do I need a jump start? Car engines sometimes need a fresh injection of energy when their batteries are flagging just to get moving again. As people, we're not so different. I find a larger than usual block of time, to step back long enough to distinguish the wood from the trees, can be a really useful way of gaining God's perspective on my like again. Not so much the last word, but the first word.

I love hillwalking, but I apologise if this analogy doesn't bless you! AW Wainwright is an unlikely hero – shy, retiring, seldom noticed. However, when I went to the Lake District recently, his wonderful guide-books to the Lakeland Fells are still the best selling books even after 50 years. They're not simple guidebooks, however, more works of art. Each guide is littered with line drawings of routes and landmarks as well as the kind of anecdotes guaranteed to brighten anyone's day in the Lakeland rain – of which there is plenty! His series of books were his life's work and the fruit of a disciplined study of the fells – he walked and sketched on the good days and wrote and planned on the bad days. Following Jesus is the journey of life for a Christian. We need rather more discipline than is popular, but it's not a route march. It's more a wonderful long walk, with Jesus leading us forward, when we respond to his voice.

Think of however many different 'bits' of your life will be helpful to provide you with an overview. Something like:

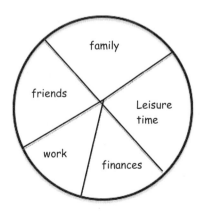

Such a picture can be a helpful starter for us re-considering what makes up our lives 24/7 and to what extent each facet reflects the character of Jesus. It's not either who we are, or what we say, but both.

Jesus must be Lord of all my life, or he cannot be Lord at all. This does not mean I have to be perfect to follow Jesus, it certainly doesn't suggest I can live the rest of my life without ever sinning, nor does it mean if I fail in any area, it's all over, but it does mean my whole life must be his. 'If Jesus is indeed God, then to truly follow Him is to pattern everything in our lives after His life.'[viii]

'Love the Lord your God with all your heart, soul, strength and mind.'

---

[i] Mark 1:17.
[ii] Dietrich Bonhoeffer, Christ the Centre, Harper Collins, San Francisco 1960, p80.
[iii] Dietrich Bonhoeffer, The Cost of Discipleship, SCM, 1948, p50.
[iv] John 14:21.
[v] 1 John 2:3
[vi] Attributed to DL Moody in response to one particular question.
[vii] Michael Frost and Alan Hirsch, Re:Jesus, Hendrikson, 2009, p79.

[viii] Follow, Floyd McClung, 2010.

THE PASSAGE for the month: Mark 1:1-20. Listen to the same passage, at least each week when you meet together. Ask where, or what, God is calling for your attention. Mark down, in the weekly table on the next page, which facet (at least one) of the following three areas of your relationships God might be speaking into:

D for discipleship – our relationship with God.
N for engagement – our relationship with others.
A for authenticity – our relationship with ourselves.

MY PRAYER FOCUS: The three people I am going to pray for, each week, this month, are:	
1	
2	
3	

MY PRACTISING: Additionally, read the material on "following" and decide what you might 'practice' to develop what it means to follow Jesus in your own life:

1. What do I need to practice this month?
It is important you decide clearly what you're going to actually do. For example, don't vaguely write 'read a book', specify which book and how much you'll read per week.

2. When do I intend to practice?
Precisely 'when'. Will it be daily, weekly, etc. If you're dependent upon opportunities arising, when will you notice them?

3. How can I ensure I do practice?
A note in your diary, a regular time in a certain place, something else needing to go to make space? Most people can't simply add more time consuming items into already too busy schedules. Do I share in my DNA group what I'm doing and ask them to ask me in x weeks time, do I put a note in the diary to ask myself? etc.

FOLLOWING – week 1.   MARK 1:1-20.

LOOK: Where in this passage is God calling for my attention?

In the light of this, what might God be saying to me in at least one facet of my life? Circle one, or more, facet of your relationships: D N A

LISTEN: What is God up to? (in my life, or those around me).

LIVE: Where have I seen God at work?

LEARN: What am I learning from my experience over the past week?

This week make sure you address this question:
'Where do I need more momentum?' in relation to 'following' Jesus this month:

ADDITIONAL NOTES ON THIS PASSAGE:

LOOK: Where in this passage is God calling for my attention?

In the light of this, what might God be saying to me in at least one facet of my life? Circle one, or more, facet of your relationships: D N A

LISTEN: What is God up to? (in my life, or those around me).

LIVE: Where have I seen God at work?

LEARN: What am I learning from my experience over the past week?

This week make sure you address this question:
What practices shall we try this month?

ADDITIONAL NOTES ON THIS PASSAGE:

LOOK: Where in this passage is God calling for my attention?

In the light of this, what might God be saying to me in at least one facet of my life? Circle one, or more, facet of your relationships: D N A

LISTEN: What is God up to? (in my life, or those around me).

LIVE: Where have I seen God at work?

LEARN: What am I learning from my experience over the past week?

This week make sure you address this question:
Who are we praying for?

ADDITIONAL NOTES ON THIS PASSAGE:

FOLLOWING – week 4.   MARK 1:1-20.

LOOK: Where in this passage is God calling for my attention?

In the light of this, what might God be saying to me in at least one facet of my life? Circle one, or more, facet of your relationships: D N A

LISTEN: What is God up to? (in my life, or those around me).

LIVE: Where have I seen God at work?

LEARN: What am I learning from my experience over the past week?

This week make sure you address this question:
How are we getting on with our practices?

ADDITIONAL NOTES ON THIS PASSAGE:

LOOK: Where, primarily over this month, in this passage is God calling for my attention?

In the light of this, what might God be saying to me in at least one facet of my life? Circle one, or more, facet of your relationships: D N A

LISTEN: What, in summary this month, is God up to? (in my life, or those around me).

LIVE: Where, pre-dominantly this month, have I seen God at work?

LEARN: What, mainly, am I learning from my experience over the past month?
Which have you circled most this month (D,N, or A)?

This week make sure you address this question:
How can we encourage one another with our practices?

ADDITIONAL NOTES ON THIS PASSAGE:

"N"GAGING

... from isolation to community.

'If you want to change society, then you must tell an alternative story.' Ivan Illich'. [i]

'It is becoming clearer every day that the most urgent problem besetting our church is this: How can we live the Christian faith in the modern world." Dietrich Bonhoeffer. [ii]

'If you talk to a man in a language he understands, that goes to his head. If you talk to him in his language, that goes to his heart.' Nelson Mandela. [iii]

From the moment Jesus said 'love your neighbour as yourself', as part of his summary on which the whole teaching of God hangs, he cemented the building of Christian community into the heart of both our practice and our message. The Church has always been intended to be an embodiment of the essential message of Jesus. Gulp! Ourselves and our relationships with one another ... 'by this everyone will know that you are my disciples, if you love one another'. [iv] The simple fact is you cannot separate Jesus' understanding of the need to love people into different compartments. Love your neighbour? Yes. Love one another already within the Church? Yes. Because of this, a DNA group itself becomes a practice ground. Your group, hopefully, soon becomes a safe environment within which you can practice. It also becomes a laboratory - where you can learn to reflect on how you get on elsewhere with other people. The thing is, none of us learn from experience automatically, despite the saying. We only actually *learn* from experiences on which we reflect upon to the pojnt when we can express what we've learnt to somebody else.

OK, so using 'eNgagement' is the corny bit - to get the letters DNA to fit what Jesus speaks about in the great commandment. Hopefully it will not simply make you stop and think, but become a frequent reminder about this vital facet of Christian living. One of today's massive challenges, within the UK, is the need for our churches to make a significant shift in their stance towards becoming missional hubs, from which we go, as opposed to worship hubs, which we merely attend. I know we can argue about how true worship isn't all about Sunday services, real worship is life 24/7, etc. but just ask yourself 'what is the organising principle of my church?' That is, what is the main principle around which we organise how we do things? Love it, or loathe it, football causes intense debate. I confess I am a passionate Liverpool fan, although after a particularly poor result, I wish I could walk away from it all. Once on the way home after a bad game, my son said, 'what number one sport shall I choose now?' All football fans have been there. However, one of the by-products I love about football, is the sense of kinship it creates immediately with total strangers (even Manchester United fans!). I've had fascinating conversations in restaurants, on trains, in queues, on the beach – basically anywhere and everywhere, once we've discovered a this shared passion. I know, I know, the same thing happens between Christians, but even at Christian celebrations I've never been enfolded in the arms of such fat, smelly blokes I don't know, as at a few crucial matches when we've scored in semi-finals and finals. Football may not be your thing (and I can pray for you about that!), but whatever your thing is, you'll, no doubt, notice a similar sense of kinship with people who share your passion. The problem, of course, for most of us is we put so much time and energy into our church commitments we just simply don't have time to get beyond the superficial with other people beyond.

I am being drawn towards the conclusion the lack of genuine engagement between existing Christians and those beyond the church, is our weakest link in the UK Church today. Most British people finding faith in Jesus today arrive as a result of a process, which takes them from unbelief, to trusting in Jesus Christ. However that process is described, or however the actual moment of 'conversion' arrives, it seems, more often than not, another person, already a follower of Jesus, is involved. The dilemmas facing many churches today are connected to the fact there is so little engagement with people who would readily follow Jesus if they knew a bit more about him. Sadly, some Christian communities seem as if they are actually designed to withdraw people from engagement with their world, rather than empower them in it. Faithful engagement in our world has become something we might get around to after our small group involvement, or worship practice, or fellowship night during the week. We know we should be engaging to truly reflect the nature of

Jesus' life and ministry, but frankly, it's much easier to send a cheque off to the latest disaster appeal and ease our conscience that way (not that this action, in and of itself is a bad idea!), but how can I become part of the solution, rather than contribute to the problem?

How do we begin to engage with other people? My suggestion is you start, although you never stop, listening to them. Whilst you may wish to choose another 'practice' to try and grow the habit of engaging others more effectively, listening to them will usually need to precede pretty much anything else. Practicing friendship is vital, showing hospitality needs to be something not simply reserved for those with the gift, intentionally planning time to be available for others is often necessary, but listening to who and where they are is essential.

Stop and think about how you become 'engaged' by others. Isn't it often the people who demonstrate an interest in you individually? How do they do that? I'm sure we all respond readily to people ready and willing to listen to us, rather than those people who are simply on the lookout for others to tell about themselves. If listening to God prepares the ground for how we follow Jesus, then listening to other people prepares the ground for how we engage with them. Combine the two practices and you're already on the road for what, I hope, will be an exciting adventure.

Notice how Jesus engages individuals throughout the gospels. If anyone could use the excuse there was too much to do it was him. Notice how Jesus usually listens before he speaks. Could we also learn to listen to people's hearts and not simply their words?

Here's some questions to think about to encourage you on your journey of listening to others:
How do I listen?
Think about some recent people you've spent time with – how much have you learnt about them, or where they might be in their lives right now?
What will I change, this week, to listen more quickly than I speak?
Who do I need to listen to this week?
What am I hearing from those I have met this week?
Do I think they feel I am listening to them?
How will I reflect on how I do/do not listen to others?

How do we discern whether the person in front of us might be waiting for Jesus himself to engage them?

If you think you are a good listener, dare to check it out by asking someone else!
'Love your neighbour as yourself'. [v] Jesus avoids categorising who our neighbour is. In telling the story of 'the good Samaritan', however, he makes it clear we can never justify drawing the circle of our engagement around ourselves too small. In practice, of course, we do just that. I confess, despite having been a Christian for over thirty years and a Christian Minister now for twenty five of them, I have only recently noticed Jesus doesn't anticipate us acting any differently - whether we're with people inside, or outside, of the Church. Oh, I realise he said 'by this love all people will recognise you are my disciples', [vi] but isn't that partly because any community oiled by the love of God is going to be noticed?

Do you ever wonder, how the Church is viewed by those beyond its boundaries? Try it out - ask some friends. Their comments will be illuminating and, if you're listening to what they're saying, it will help you and hopefully your church, with engaging them. The old adage, 'you may be the only Bible some people will ever read' is a reflection of at least two things:
-   The fact the Church, in general terms, is disconnected from the rest of society.
-   The potential for ordinary Christians (if such a thing exists) to make a profound impact.

To what extent are we the salt and light Jesus speaks about? Whatever else Jesus is saying here, he anticipates salt being in connection with whatever requires it and light not being covered. Most people in DNA groups find the challenge to pray regularly for three people who are not yet Christians, a big problem. To begin praying for three people, not yet Christians, brings home the realisation, for many, we have very few friends beyond the Church. Most Christians, at present in the UK, have little depth of relationship with at least three people, who are not yet Christians. Whilst a Carol Service remains the easiest Christian event to invite a friend along to, most of us don't see any response. Certainly, among the network of Churches

I am a part of, our attendance overall at Christmas is less than double our regular attendance at Christian worship.

Maybe we need to pray for God to guide us to people for whom we can pray! To then ask 'am I the answer to the prayers of those around me' becomes a prayer designed to take us out of our comfort zone. You can't be friends with everyone. Consider this table:

Number	People	Type of engagement
1	John	Seemingly Jesus' best and closest friend - 'the beloved disciple.'
3	Peter, James & John	A few closer friends. These three would appear to have shared more with Jesus, even among the twelve, than others.
12	The twelve disciples	A small group of good friends. Evidently, disciples and friends – including Judas (who didn't take Jesus by surprise).
72	cf. Luke 10	A larger group where he was known and able to share more of life than with casual acquaintances. The wider group of followers Jesus assembled. He taught them, but their 'networks' were primarily elsewhere.
150 approx.	cf. Acts 1:12-15 – was this 'about 120' (verse 15) and the 11 disciples, and the 'women and Mary and Jesus' brothers?'	Those whom relationship with Jesus brought together – including family. The group(s) he most connected with. Somewhere between 120 and 150 were still 'with Jesus' as a group at the beginning of Acts and prepared to 'wait' for the next initiative of the Holy Spirit on the day of Pentecost.
???	The 'crowd'	Anyone who listened, or observed Jesus life in a more than superficial manner. The wider group who came under the influence of Jesus teaching and life. No known figures can be set on this group which varied from place to place.

How does this kind of pattern feature in your own life right now? If Jesus, developed different levels of friendship with different people, surely this potentially frees us from treating everyone the same also. Jesus engaged with everyone he met, but he didn't actually have time for everyone according to their own expectations.

---

[i] This was the response, attributed to Ivan Illich, in response to the question: 'What is the most revolutionary way to change society: Is it violent revolution, or is it gradual reform?'

[ii] Dietrich Bonhoeffer. The Cost of Discipleship. SCM London 1959. This was one of Bonhoeffer's most significant books translated from the original Nachfolge – first published in German in 1937! If he was right and this was an urgent matter then, what about now?

[iii] Nelson Mandela, reported quote, source unknown.
[iv] John 13:35.
[v] Luke 10: 27.
[vi] John 13: 35.

THE PASSAGE for the month: Luke 10:1-12. Listen to the same passage, at least each week when you meet together. Ask where, or what, God is calling for your attention. Mark down, in the weekly table on the next page, which facet (at least one) of the following three areas of your relationships God might be speaking into:

D for discipleship – our relationship with God.
N for engagement – our relationship with others.
A for authenticity – our relationship with ourselves.

MY PRAYER FOCUS: The three people I am going to pray for, each week, this month, are:	
1	
2	
3	

MY PRACTISING: Additionally, read the material on "engaging" and consider what you might 'practice' to develop what it means to engage more meaningfully with others in your own life:

1. What do I need to practice this month?
It is important you decide clearly what you're going to actually do. For example, don't vaguely write 'read a book', specify which book and how much you'll read per week.

2. When do I intend to practice?
Precisely 'when'. Will it be daily, weekly, etc. If you're dependent upon opportunities arising, when will you notice them?

3. How can I ensure I do practice?
A note in your diary, a regular time in a certain place, something else needing to go to make space? Most people can't simply add more time consuming items into already too busy schedules. Do I share in my DNA group what I'm doing and ask them to ask me in x weeks time, do I put a note in the diary to ask myself? etc.

LOOK: Where in this passage is God calling for my attention?

In the light of this, what might God be saying to me in at least one facet of my life? Circle one, or more, facet of your relationships: D N A

LISTEN: What is God up to? (in my life, or those around me).

LIVE: Where have I seen God at work?

LEARN: What am I learning from my experience over the past week?

This week make sure you address this question:
'Where do I need more momentum?' in relation to 'following' Jesus this month:

ADDITIONAL NOTES ON THIS PASSAGE:

LOOK: Where in this passage is God calling for my attention?

In the light of this, what might God be saying to me in at least one facet of my life? Circle one, or more, facet of your relationships: D N A

LISTEN: What is God up to? (in my life, or those around me).

LIVE: Where have I seen God at work?

LEARN: What am I learning from my experience over the past week?

This week make sure you address this question:
What practices shall we try this month?

ADDITIONAL NOTES ON THIS PASSAGE:

LOOK: Where in this passage is God calling for my attention?

In the light of this, what might God be saying to me in at least one facet of my life? Circle one, or more, facet of your relationships: D N A

LISTEN: What is God up to? (in my life, or those around me).

LIVE: Where have I seen God at work?

LEARN: What am I learning from my experience over the past week?

This week make sure you address this question:
Who are we praying for?

ADDITIONAL NOTES ON THIS PASSAGE:

LOOK: Where in this passage is God calling for my attention?

In the light of this, what might God be saying to me in at least one facet of my life? Circle one, or more, facet of your relationships: D N A

LISTEN: What is God up to? (in my life, or those around me).

LIVE: Where have I seen God at work?

LEARN: What am I learning from my experience over the past week?

This week make sure you address this question:
How are we getting on with our practices?

ADDITIONAL NOTES ON THIS PASSAGE:

LOOK: Where, primarily over this month, in this passage is God calling for my attention?

In the light of this, what might God be saying to me in at least one facet of my life? Circle one, or more, facet of your relationships: D N A

LISTEN: What, in summary this month, is God up to? (in my life, or those around me).

LIVE: Where, pre-dominantly this month, have I seen God at work?

LEARN: What, mainly, am I learning from my experience over the past month?
Which have you circled most this month (D,N, or A)?

This week make sure you address this question:
How can we encourage one another with our practices?

ADDITIONAL NOTES ON THIS PASSAGE:

AUTHENTICITY

.... from fragmentation to integrity.

'If it acts like a duck (all the time), it's a duck. Doesn't matter if the duck thinks it's a dog, it's still a duck as far as the rest of us are concerned. Authenticity is doing what you promise, not being wh you are.' Seth Godin. [i]

"Basically, I'm always looking for a place – for somewhere to be." – Paul Tournier. [ii]

'Jesus yes, the church no' – that was the piece of graffiti made famous in the 1960's. By no means was this the beginning, but it did herald a new boldness to the challenge and accusation towards the church: 'hypocrites!' We are all, to varying degrees, let's face it, hypocrites. No one fully measures up against the life of Jesus. I like Tony Campolo's response to this accusation best, when he simply says 'come and join us then, you'll feel very much at home among us'. [iii] None of us, in actual fact, even live up to our own expectations. The change in the air in our generation, is it is not simply those opposed to Christianity who are voicing 'Jesus yes, the church no'. There is a growing dis-ease within the church itself. It would be the easiest thing in the world to look around and find someone else to blame, but surely our challenge is to find some pathways whereby we can be part of the answer, rather than part of the problem. Closing the gap, or void between who we are and who we say we are may well be the greatest challenge facing the people of God, in the UK, today. Our authenticity is at stake. Sadly, in the eyes of those outside the kingdom of God, this means the plausibility of God is at stake too.

With gold we can look for the hallmark to discover it's authenticity as a precious metal. With diamonds it takes a closer, skilled examination to determine whether it's a genuine stone, or not. I love the story in Alexander McCall Smith's No 1 Ladies Detective Agency series when Mma Ramotswe and JLB Maketoni reach the point of deciding to buy an engagement ring (he rather unwillingly it has to be said). Each of them, independently, question the integrity of the diamond-seller and so they set out to get the ring exchanged for the genuine article. Consequently, whilst one exchanges the fake with a real diamond ring the other, inadvertently, switches it back, leaving them with the fake again!

The often said challenge that we may be the only Bible many people ever read is one we need to face and come to terms with – for the sake of those around us.

Do you see your DNA group as both a gift and an opportunity yet? Jesus says 'where two or three come together in my name, there I am with them' [1] I usually hear this verse spoken in prayer, when I'm the visiting speaker, as an apology, for there being fewer people than anticipated! People quote it to boost the morale of the few, but Jesus meant what he said! He's not saying 'only when there are two or three' and absents himself when there are more, but neither does he imply he is more present when there are more people. Is this, therefore, the essential building block for the Church – maybe not as we know it, but as Jesus anticipated? As TS Eliot once posed the question: 'What is life if you have not life together?' [2]

When we meet the authentic, real, genuine, fully God and man, fully present, Christ is with us! When we meet together, therefore, we need to see it as an opportunity to meet with Jesus, not simply around his words. 'I am with you always, to the very end of the age' [3] tells us Jesus commits himself to be with us. Just imagine, what if when Jesus says, 'for where two, or three come together in my name, there I am with them' he actually means what he says! [iv] A DNA group provides the environment in which we can practice being the authentic followers of Jesus we have been born, by the Spirit of God, to be. If you cannot admit our failings and sin with two other followers of Jesus, then how much harder will it be to acknowledge you are less than perfect when with others? Our friends and colleagues know this already. It's more likely to be the way we pretend to be someone else which puts people off, than being real. 'I came to see he was just like me and realised if Jesus could accept him, then he might accept me too' - I've heard this so many times. [v] Also, think about what admitting your failings does for you positively. You begin to learn you can trust other people not to turn their back simply because you don't measure up – acceptance by other people for who we really are, is a

---

[1] Matthew 18:20.

[2] TS Eliot, Choruses from "The Rock" in 'Collected Poems 1909-62', Faber 1974.

[3] Matthew 28: 20.

wonderful gift to treasure, but we'll only find it if we risk it. Not only do I find it sometimes easier to accept God's forgiveness once I've spoken something out aloud to someone else, but the invitation given for someone to ask me how I'm getting on with it next week provides me with a helpful sense of accountability. Kept to myself I more easily fall down again.

How on earth can we ever become more authentic followers of Jesus? This is such an important question I encourage you to grapple with, but you'll probably already know, it's one we'd rather avoid. The practice I'm suggesting you work at, unless you can find something more appropriate for where you are in your adventure with God, is what is grandly termed 'the prayer of examen'. In essence it's about listening to ourselves in the presence of God and helps us develop a rhythm of self-accountability with Him.

We owe much to St Ignatius of Loyola and Jesuit Spirituality for this particular gift and it has two basic aspects:

i. An examen of *consciousness* through which we discover how God has been present to us throughout the day and how we have responded to his loving presence.
    When doing this we may simply be recalling things we noticed at the time, but we may be opening our heart to ways in which God was working, although we were unaware in those moments. Make it your own, but recognise the greatest benefit will be found by finding a regular rhythm – so, for example, if praying alone works best for you daily in the mornings, reviewing the previous day may be your preferred option. Some good questions might be:
    When did I sense your presence the most in my day?
    When did your presence seem farthest away from me in my day?
    How were you expressing your love in my day?
    How were you loving me, even when your presence seemed far away?
    How did I respond to your love in my day?

i. An examen of *conscience* in which we uncover those areas that need cleansing, purifying and healing.

Here we allow God to search our heart. We're not trying to make ourselves miserable by highlighting every sinful fault and failing, but open ourselves to God in the light of the truth in our own heart. Of course, even if our experience highlights the reality of sin, this in itself is helpful - we can acknowledge our need for forgiveness and inner cleansing – and be better equipped when we face the same situation again. Some areas of exploration could be:

Are any idols drawing the attention of my heart?

Are there any unhealthy attachments?

Are there particular things I'm struggling with?

Where are my desires and beliefs not directed by God?

Which sins do I need to confess?

It is, therefore, intended as a regular practice, which enables us to sift our motivations and actions with the intention of bringing more shalom, or integrity, to the living out of our life of faith.

1. **Remember** – you are in the presence of God. Some means of consciously acknowledging this fact is essential. "Lord I offer once again my very self in your presence."

2. **Thanksgiving** – look over your day with gratitude for the gifts it has brought. What are you most grateful for in this day? In what ways have I experienced the love of God? "Lord I thank you for helping me experience your love in this day."

3. **Ask** – the Holy Spirit to help you look at your actions and attitudes. "Lord. I invite you to shine the spotlight of your Holy Spirit in my heart and help me to see more of what you see."

4. **Reflect** - what has been going on for you below the surface? Examine yourself Where have you responded positively to the gifts of God and where have you been hesitant? Where was your heart divided – between helping and disregarding, listening and ignoring, or speaking and silence? Have you recognised the presence of God in the midst of your attitudes and actions? etc. Take your time here. "Lord, what were you looking to be up to?"

5. **Heart-to-heart** – leave space for the opportunity to share your innermost thoughts and feelings with Jesus. Maybe it is forgiveness you require, or en expression of sorrow, gratitude, joy, need, help, etc. "My Lord and my God."

What is my responsibility? It is easy to be drawn to one end of the spectrum, or the other when it comes to the issue of responsibility. We may veer towards the 'let go and let God' school of discipleship, or the 'wear out, don't rust out' school, but whilst both can find some biblical support, either to an extreme avoids the creative biblical tension I believe God intended us to live in. Clearly (at least to my mind) God takes responsibility for all he needs to, but this does not remove the element of delegated responsibility for human beings created in his likeness (that is, all of us).

Think about it for a moment. Until we accept our own personal responsibility for the reality of sin in our own lives, we don't, in practice, receive the forgiveness Jesus offers to us. Previous generations, in the UK, didn't need to be told they were 'sinners' – they were only too well aware of this. However, our generation struggles with owning sin - partly because the word has dropped out of everyday usage, partly because our awareness of God has diminished, but also because we are so adept at blaming somebody else. We blame the hospital when somebody dies. We blame the parents when somebody is committed for murder. We blame our background when we want to justify inappropriate behaviour. We blame the other driver because our insurance company tells us to. We blame the multi-national company because we didn't read the small print. Examples are everywhere – just listen carefully to today's news and you'll hear them.
There is, however, a positive side to this equation. Becoming a follower of Jesus enables us to take appropriate personal responsibility.

Work out what is God's responsibility, what belongs to somebody else and what is yours.

Only when you have differentiated between where responsibility lies can you begin to do something about it.

- If it's God's: give whatever it is to him.
- If it belongs with someone else: leave it with them.
- If it's appropriately within your power to do something about: accept it.

---

[i] Seth Godin's blog entry 16th. February 2009. He makes the point Motehr Teresa was often filled with self-doubt, but was an authentic saint because she acted like one. His books are well worth reading.

[iii] Simply from my notes from his preaching.

[iv] Matthew 18:20.

[v] I suggest you begin to listen to the stories of those who have come to faith recently. I'm confident you'll hear this same theme from many people.

THE PASSAGE for this month: Matthew 5:1-16 is this month's passage. Listen to the same passage, at least each week when you meet together, asking where, or what, God is calling for your attention. Mark down, in the weekly table on the next page, which facet (at least one) of the following three areas of your relationships God might be speaking into:

D for discipleship – our relationship with God.
N for engagement – our relationship with others.
A for authenticity – our relationship with ourselves.

MY PRAYER FOCUS: The three people I am going to pray for, each week, this month, are:	
1	
2	
3	

MY PRACTISING: Additionally, read the material on "authenticity" and consider what you might 'practice' to develop what it means to engage more meaningfully with others in your own life:

1. What do I need to practice this month?
It is important you decide clearly what you're going to actually do. For example, don't vaguely write 'read a book', specify which book and how much you'll read per week.

2. When do I intend to practice?
Precisely 'when'. Will it be daily, weekly, etc. If you're dependent upon opportunities arising, when will you notice them?

3. How can I ensure I do practice?
A note in your diary, a regular time in a certain place, something else needing to go to make space? Most people can't simply add more time consuming items into already too busy schedules. Do I share in my DNA group what I'm doing and ask them to ask me in x weeks time, do I put a note in the diary to ask myself? etc.

AUTHENTICITY - week 1.   MATTHEW 5:1-16.

LOOK: Where in this passage is God calling for my attention?

In the light of this, what might God be saying to me in at least one facet of my life? Circle one, or more, facet of your relationships: D N A

LISTEN: What is God up to? (in my life, or those around me).

LIVE: Where have I seen God at work?

LEARN: What am I learning from my experience over the past week?

This week make sure you address this question:
'Where do I need more momentum?' in relation to 'following' Jesus this month:

ADDITIONAL NOTES ON THIS PASSAGE:

AUTHENTICITY – week 2.   **MATTHEW 5:1-16.**

LOOK: Where in this passage is God calling for my attention?

In the light of this, what might God be saying to me in at least one facet of my life? Circle one, or more, facet of your relationships: D N A

LISTEN: What is God up to? (in my life, or those around me).

LIVE: Where have I seen God at work?

LEARN: What am I learning from my experience over the past week?

This week make sure you address this question:
What practices shall we try this month?

ADDITIONAL NOTES ON THIS PASSAGE:

LOOK: Where in this passage is God calling for my attention?

In the light of this, what might God be saying to me in at least one facet of my life? Circle one, or more, facet of your relationships: D N A

LISTEN: What is God up to? (in my life, or those around me).

LIVE: Where have I seen God at work?

LEARN: What am I learning from my experience over the past week?

This week make sure you address this question:
Who are we praying for?

ADDITIONAL NOTES ON THIS PASSAGE:

LOOK: Where in this passage is God calling for my attention?

In the light of this, what might God be saying to me in at least one facet of my life? Circle one, or more, facet of your relationships: D N A

LISTEN: What is God up to? (in my life, or those around me).

LIVE: Where have I seen God at work?

LEARN: What am I learning from my experience over the past week?

This week make sure you address this question:
How are we getting on with our practices?

ADDITIONAL NOTES ON THIS PASSAGE:

LOOK: Where, primarily over this month, in this passage is God calling for my attention?

In the light of this, what might God be saying to me in at least one facet of my life? Circle one, or more, facet of your relationships: D N A

LISTEN: What, in summary this month, is God up to? (in my life, or those around me).

LIVE: Where, pre-dominantly this month, have I seen God at work?

LEARN: What, mainly, am I learning from my experience over the past month?
Which have you circled most this month (D,N, or A)?

This week make sure you address this question:
How can we encourage one another with our practices?

ADDITIONAL NOTES ON THIS PASSAGE:

LEARNING

... from information to formation.

'Where is the wisdom we have lost in knowledge?' – TS Eliot. [i]

'No one learns anything from experience – we only learn from experience on which we reflect and are then able to articulate to others.' – Pat Keifert. [ii]

'He who dares to teach, must never cease to learn.' [iii]

This month, we shall continue with downloading what it means to be a disciple into our everyday living. Following was first, now learning.

Sharpening the saw.
Suppose you were to come across someone in the woods working feverishly to saw down a tree.
"What are you doing?" you ask.
"Can't you see", comes the impatient reply. "I'm sawing down this tree".
"You look exhausted!" you exclaim. "How long have you been at it?"
"Over five hours," he says, " and I'm whacked out. This is really tough work."
"Well why don't you take a break for a few minutes and sharpen that saw?"
"I don't have time to sharpen the saw," the man says emphatically. "I'm too busy sawing!"

The first time I heard this story I noted it down - thinking it would be a useful illustration for a sermon. Eventually, I acknowledged, it was speaking to me, rather more clearly than I really wanted to admit. I keep coming back to consider its truth, time and time again. My guess is I'm not alone in needing to hear what's being said here, so I'd encourage you to stop and reflect on your own life for a few minutes before you rush on. If we don't stop, we don't learn and a disciple is a learner – always! (You never lose the 'L' plates).

I once began to start thinking God only ever spoke to Christians when they went on holiday! So many people came back having heard God speak 'more clearly than ever'. Of course, that's partly the point of any form of retreat, but God is speaking continually. It is simply I am, too often, too busy to notice. How about you?

Ask yourself the question 'what is a disciple of Jesus all about?' Even Before becoming a Christian, I think I'd heard 'a learner' was something to do with being a disciple. Maybe I picked up the idea at school, but it is certainly of the essence of meaning behind the word 'disciple'. However, growing up thinking that learning was all about school, didn't really excite me about following in the footsteps of Jesus and being his disciple. My hunch is he'd not have been too thrilled about my school either, if that's what they taught! The good news is learning is not the same as acquiring knowledge. Phew!

Maggie and I realised we were middle-aged when we started wanting to stay in to watch the gardening programme rather than venture out on a Friday night!. Am I a gardener? Well, I have a garden, which seems to be an essential bit of the equipment, but watching others do something you're interested in does not equal becoming a gardener anymore than sitting in a church worship service automatically translates what you hear into the action of your own life. Most of our gardening has been and remains trial and error. Truth is, you learn little from a book, or even a step-by-step Alan Titchmarsh programme. The main way Maggie and I have learnt anything about gardening (believe me, it's not a lot) is when we've stopped and thought about why something has worked/grown, or (more often) not! We've learnt more from our mistakes than we have our successes. My best advice for anyone, interested in gardening is: start digging! Want to follow Jesus? Start walking!

Part of the good news, in the process of learning to follow Jesus, is the realisation I don't need to *know* anywhere near as much I thought, in order to be a real disciple of Jesus Christ. Very often, we think we need to know more information before we do more. Just think back to when you first became a Christian, or ask yourself: 'who are the most fruitful and effective disciples at present in my church?' If I was a betting man, I'd be putting money on the answer being those who have most recently come to know Jesus. Have another look at Luke chapters 9 & 10 where Jesus sends out, firstly, the twelve and, subsequently, the fruit of chapter 9, the seventy-two. Ask yourself, how much knowledge did they actually have before Jesus trusted them to live out and proclaim the kingdom of God? Jesus was an apprentice carpenter for more of his human life than he was a preacher – he didn't simply learn carpentry however.

It was a Sunday evening and I was clearly spoken to by God: 'go and speak with Tim'. I'd been putting it off for a while, even though I sensed he was interested in exploring faith in God, I just needed to do something about it. The problem was, it was now the next Sunday, same place, same time, but nothing had taken place. Good intentions – don't you just love them!

So, if I were to ask you what are you learning? How would you answer? If panic begins to set in at the very thought of someone asking, I suggest you have yet to absorb the fact that learning is not something you simply get out of a textbook. How, though, do we move round what is often referred to as the 'learning-reflection cycle'.

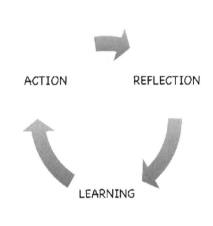

ACTION   REFLECTION

LEARNING

When have I learnt I am overweight? (just one example of the learning-reflection cycle).

I am not willing to acnowldge this is affecting me in any way.
I am out of breath when I run up the stairs.
I am conscious overweight might be an issue for my overall health.
I am weighing myself on the scales.
I am thinking of doing something about it.
I am watching a good TV series on health and weight.
I am trying to lose weight, unsuccessfully.
I am trying to lose weight with some success, but not sure how.
I am attending a weight watchers course.
I am reading more about exercise, health and weight loss.
I have set some targets for losing weight.
I have reached my optimum weight.
I am feeling much healthier.

I am advocating weight loss to my friends.
I am explaining my story to a friend.

You repeat the cycle, not to always to develop a new idea, but improve & develop the original one. I think of this as 'stop-to-act', which reminds me how my thinking and doing are linked. The cycle demonstrates the clear links between action, reflection & change.

trial - new experience in reality.

observation & reflection

new idea, or thought.

practising new idea

You can start wherever you wish, but the real learning comes with completing a cycle.

Some of us keep making the same mistakes because we never stop to reflect on what we're doing and why. Some of us are keeping our light under a bushel: we actually do know a lot about many things, but either we don't realise it, or no one else does, because we never dare speak it out.
So, where's your barrier with whatever you're seeking to learn next? This is something which can apply to everything and I hope you'll look to develop the habit, or try again, to practise it during this year. You can't practice anything by simply learning a theory. Faith is something you can learn little about by talking with one another - you personally wont learn very much yourself until to try it out in practice.
The kind of faith Jesus is interested in growing within us all is one we practise – not because of some bizarre heavenly challenge, but because he knows we'll only grow it through practice. Also, he wants

THE PASSAGE for this month: John 15:1-27 is this month's passage. Listen to the same passage, at least each week when you meet together, asking where, or what, God is calling for your attention. Mark down, in the weekly table on the next page, which facet (at least one) of the following three areas of your relationships God might be speaking into:

D for discipleship – our relationship with God.
N for engagement – our relationship with others.
A for authenticity – our relationship with ourselves.

MY PRAYER FOCUS: The three people I am going to pray for, each week, this month, are:	
1	
2	
3	

MY PRACTISING: Additionally, read the material on "learning" and consider what you might 'practice' to develop what it means to engage more meaningfully with others in your own life:

1. What do I need to practice this month?
It is important you decide clearly what you're going to actually do. For example, don't vaguely write 'read a book', specify which book and how much you'll read per week.

2. When do I intend to practice?
Precisely 'when'. Will it be daily, weekly, etc. If you're dependent upon opportunities arising, when will you notice them?

3. How can I ensure I do practice?
A note in your diary, a regular time in a certain place, something else needing to go to make space? Most people can't simply add more time consuming items into already too busy schedules. Do I share in my DNA group what I'm doing and ask them to ask me in x weeks time, do I put a note in the diary to ask myself? etc.

LOOK:　　　Where in this passage is God calling for my attention?

In the light of this, what might God be saying to me in at least one facet of my life? Circle one, or more, facet of your relationships: D N A

LISTEN:　　What is God up to? (in my life, or those around me).

LIVE:　　　Where have I seen God at work?

LEARN:　　What am I learning from my experience over the past week?

This week make sure you address this question:
'Where do I need more momentum?' in relation to 'following' Jesus this month:

ADDITIONAL NOTES ON THIS PASSAGE:

LOOK: Where in this passage is God calling for my attention?

In the light of this, what might God be saying to me in at least one facet of my life? Circle one, or more, facet of your relationships: D N A

LISTEN: What is God up to? (in my life, or those around me).

LIVE: Where have I seen God at work?

LEARN: What am I learning from my experience over the past week?

This week make sure you address this question:
What practices shall we try this month?

ADDITIONAL NOTES ON THIS PASSAGE:

LOOK: Where in this passage is God calling for my attention?

In the light of this, what might God be saying to me in at least one facet of my life? Circle one, or more, facet of your relationships: D N A

LISTEN: What is God up to? (in my life, or those around me).

LIVE: Where have I seen God at work?

LEARN: What am I learning from my experience over the past week?

This week make sure you address this question:
Who are we praying for?

ADDITIONAL NOTES ON THIS PASSAGE:

LOOK: Where in this passage is God calling for my attention?

In the light of this, what might God be saying to me in at least one facet of my life? Circle one, or more, facet of your relationships: D N A

LISTEN: What is God up to? (in my life, or those around me).

LIVE: Where have I seen God at work?

LEARN: What am I learning from my experience over the past week?

This week make sure you address this question:
How are we getting on with our practices?

ADDITIONAL NOTES ON THIS PASSAGE:

LOOK: Where, primarily over this month, in this passage is God calling for my attention?

In the light of this, what might God be saying to me in at least one facet of my life? Circle one, or more, facet of your relationships: D N A

LISTEN: What, in summary this month, is God up to? (in my life, or those around me).

LIVE: Where, pre-dominantly this month, have I seen God at work?

LEARN: What, mainly, am I learning from my experience over the past month?
Which have you circled most this month (D,N, or A)?

This week make sure you address this question:
How can we encourage one another with our practices?

ADDITIONAL NOTES ON THIS PASSAGE:

AUTHENTICITY – week 1.   MATTHEW 5:1-16.

LOOK: Where in this passage is God calling for my attention?

In the light of this, what might God be saying to me in at least one facet of my life? Circle one, or more, facet of your relationships: D N A

LISTEN: What is God up to? (in my life, or those around me).

LIVE: Where have I seen God at work?

LEARN: What am I learning from my experience over the past week?

This week make sure you address this question:
'Where do I need more momentum?' in relation to 'following' Jesus this month:

ADDITIONAL NOTES ON THIS PASSAGE:

LOOK: Where in this passage is God calling for my attention?

In the light of this, what might God be saying to me in at least one facet of my life? Circle one, or more, facet of your relationships: D N A

LISTEN: What is God up to? (in my life, or those around me).

LIVE: Where have I seen God at work?

LEARN: What am I learning from my experience over the past week?

This week make sure you address this question:
What practices shall we try this month?

ADDITIONAL NOTES ON THIS PASSAGE:

AUTHENTICITY - week 3.   MATTHEW 5:1-16.

LOOK: Where in this passage is God calling for my attention?

In the light of this, what might God be saying to me in at least one facet
of my life? Circle one, or more, facet of your relationships: D N A

LISTEN: What is God up to? (in my life, or those around me).

LIVE: Where have I seen God at work?

LEARN: What am I learning from my experience over the past week?

This week make sure you address this question:
Who are we praying for?

ADDITIONAL NOTES ON THIS PASSAGE:

AUTHENTICITY – week 4.   MATTHEW 5:1-16.

LOOK: Where in this passage is God calling for my attention?

In the light of this, what might God be saying to me in at least one facet of my life? Circle one, or more, facet of your relationships: D N A

LISTEN: What is God up to? (in my life, or those around me).

LIVE: Where have I seen God at work?

LEARN: What am I learning from my experience over the past week?

This week make sure you address this question:
How are we getting on with our practices?

ADDITIONAL NOTES ON THIS PASSAGE:

LOOK: Where, primarily over this month, in this passage is God calling for my attention?

In the light of this, what might God be saying to me in at least one facet of my life? Circle one, or more, facet of your relationships: D N A

LISTEN: What, in summary this month, is God up to? (in my life, or those around me).

LIVE: Where, pre-dominantly this month, have I seen God at work?

LEARN: What, mainly, am I learning from my experience over the past month?
Which have you circled most this month (D,N, or A)?

This week make sure you address this question:
How can we encourage one another with our practices?

ADDITIONAL NOTES ON THIS PASSAGE:

AVAILABILITY

.... from busyness to availability.

'I place no value on anything I possess, except in relation to the Kingdom of God.' David Livingstone.

'Being has to express itself in doing.' Jacques Ellul. [i]

Availability is a precious gift – when you're on the receiving end. However, if you're offering someone else your time, making yourself available to them, it often feels as if you're giving nothing.

This story is sobering, because whilst the names of the people involved may be unknown, their responses will not be. The World Book Encyclopedia describes Charles Francis Adams, the son of President John Quincy Adams, as "one of the most successful diplomats in United States history." He gained this reputation through his work here in the UK between 1861 and 1868. The encyclopedia makes no mention of his family, but Charles' diary does. One day's entry reads: "Went fishing today with my son— a day wasted." However, another diary gives a different perspective: "Went fishing with my father—the most wonderful day in my life!" The person who wrote these words was Charles' son, Brook. Commitment to our children, or any other human being, is not expressed on a single day, but in the culmination of a lifelong series of smaller, daily actions. I hear, sadly most frequently from Christian leaders, people talk about 'quality time' with their spouse, or their children. Anyone who's married to a workaholic, however, will tell you they'd rather have more quantity than feel as if they're given just another slot of an hour in their spouses diary – however good the meal is!

I'd prepare yourself for an uncomfortable month! If you're daring to take a closer look at your availability for others becoming a noticeable habit of your life then it will, if you're anything like most people, be a challenging experience.

Seriously, stop and ask yourself the question 'how much time am I available for others?' We are constantly making choices about how we use our time. The most frequently cited reason, for not being able to do most things, is "I don't have time". Interestingly, I use this excuse both for things I really want to do in my leisure time (such as travelling to watch Liverpool, or playing golf), as well as things I put off and really ought to do in my work time.

	Sun	Mon	Tues	Weds	Thurs	Fri	Sat
8am							
9am							
10am							
11am							
12am							
1pm							
2pm							
3pm							
4pm							
5pm							
6pm							
7pm							
8pm							
9pm							
10pm							

Fill in the blanks with what you were doing last week. Take note of what patterns you see and take time to answer some questions:

Such as: is what is important to me finding enough time? When am I with others? How available am I? Is there any space for someone else without needing to plan it in? Is there any time for people who are not yet Christians? Are there things I don't really need to do, or be at? How much happens to me and how much do I decide to make happen? Are there any gaps? Is something crucial missing?

If you don't find time to do this simple exercise within a couple of weeks, you're too busy! How many people say on their deathbed 'I wish I'd spent more time at the office?'

Of course, observing what's going on is not the same as doing something about it. I suggest you dare to share, however much of your findings you wish, with your DNA group. Afterwards, decide upon one thing you will change about your typical week. Don't try not to change too much too soon, rather aim at do-able incremental changes one at a time. Also, it may be you don't need to fit everything into your weekly schedule –some things might find a better place monthly.

Jesus talks about Christians needing to be both salt and light. [1] He also talks about the kingdom of God being like both a mustard seed and yeast. [2] Something all these analogies have in common is their need to be in close proximity, in order to be effective. Salt brings no flavour remaining in the bag. Light offers no illumination hidden from sight. Seeds don't grow if not planted. Yeast only releases its power when mixed in. My conviction is Jesus sees engagement with our neighbor as being part of the DNA for every Christian. Read the gospels, study the life of Jesus – he wasn't simply around other people, he engaged with them.

Not only have all human beings been created in God's image, we have been created for relationship. Even God himself exists in trinity, in relationship, Father, Son and Holy Spirit. Relationship is of the very essence of God himself! It follows, therefore, as disciples of Jesus, relationships will form part of the very flow of the life of the kingdom of God. To engage, or not engage, seems to be the question. Our crowded diaries, leave no space for real engagement and conspire against any meaningful proximity between followers of Jesus and other people existing. The single greatest weakness in the UK Church today? Whilst I spend a lot of time talking with leaders of Churches about vision, strategy, mission, values and similar concerns, I'm drawn towards the conclusion most of our church organisation merely works to keep us away from where God most needs us to be – with other people. In 'Finding Faith Today' it was recognized, 7 out of every 10 people coming to faith in Jesus cited the main factor, in their journey to faith, as being another person. [3] My sense is, with the landscape of society changing so much, subsequently, that is probably even higher today.

I recall Cath, talking about her friends and how they'd become very

---

[1] Matthew 5: 13-16.
[2] Luke 13: 18-21.
[3] Finding Faith Today, John Finney, British and Foreign Bible Society, 1992. p36.

interested in her new-found faith in Jesus. No one had taught her about 'evangelism', she hardly knew anything about the contents of the Bible, but stuff happened simply because she spent enough time with enough other people. How many more encounters with Jesus, mediated through a Christian, are just waiting to happen? Maybe some of your friends are among them.

"You don't get what you expect, you only get what you inspect." I heard these words quoted in relation to the whole subject of delegation and team leading. I think they hold a load of truth. However, when I began to apply them personally I soon realised their main benefit is to be found when I take time out to inspect my own life, rather than the performance of others! Setting myself some high expectations is one thing, but saying 'yes' to unrealisable goals merely sets me up for unnecessary disappointment. When it's disappointment, brought on myself, because from the moment of saying 'yes' failure was inevitable, is just plain stupid. Why? Intentionality, which translates into planning, if not present, usually means most people's targets, or goals, are missed because they never have a chance.

Maggie: 'We're out of the habit of hospitality, don't you think we ought to invite some people around for a meal.'
Nigel: 'Absolutely, I've been thinking the same myself, let's do it.'
Three months later, Maggie, or Nigel: 'You remember we agreed we need to invite more people around for meals, don't you think we need to start again?'

Sadly, this is not a made up conversation, nor have the names been changed to protect anonymity! Maggie and I have such conversations regularly and not simply about one subject. We agree on a lot, many things we both think are not just good ideas, but fit well with who we are. We even both really enjoy welcoming people into our home, sitting down, eating good food (admittedly this part of the equation has nothing to do with me) with friends. The tragedy is, unless we plan some time, keep it free from other possibilities (even before we know who we'll invite), it doesn't usually happen. Is there any space in your diary for God to simply surprise you, or have you effectively put out the 'no vacancies' sign to the rest of your world?

Over the course of a year, hopefully, everyone in a DNA group gradually identifies at least three people they will particularly pray for. Of itself, this is a huge challenge and most of us start by thinking 'I don't know three people not yet Christians well enough'. However, you are the answer to the prayers of the people around you! Maybe like me, you instinctively recoil from such a statement. So when Maggie told me she'd offered another couple *we* would decorate a room in their house, because they weren't able to do that themselves, I found many good reasons why not, until I remembered these words, I'd heard elsewhere. In the end I both enjoyed it and found it immensely rewarding, but I couldn't have done it without saying 'no' to other grabs for my diary. All I'm suggesting is, we place the people we're praying for, alongside making ourselves available to them and see what happens. If you make no time, then 'nothing' is the most likely result.

Becoming the answer to the prayers of the people around you can easily sound like arrogance to those of us who are British brought up on a strict diet of humble pie. But think about it, before you dismiss it. What is it most people are praying for? Rather than a simple relief of symptoms, people are searching for something deeper. When people are struggling with ill health they look for support before they look for a cure, when they lose their job they need a friend before they start looking for another job, etc. As you begin to get to know people, you'll discover they have deeper questions and whilst you might not have all the intellectual answers ready to hand, you can 'always be prepared to give an answer to everyone who asks you to give a reason for the hope that you have.' [4]

What can we practice to develop availability? I suggest you start by making sure you spend enough time with enough people for questions to arise in your conversation.

There are two great things about asking questions:

    i.   You don't need to know anything before you begin.
   ii.   You do end up learning a great deal.

---

[4] 1 Peter 3: 15.

In some ways these highlight the barriers to asking questions:

i.   Pride – we feel like idiots because we think everyone else knows the answer.
ii. Embarrassment – we feel we should know the answer.
iii. Arrogance – we don't want to admit we don't know the answer.

My guess is most of us know rather too much about pride, embarrassment and arrogance and we would benefit from a little less of each around our lives – so look on the bright side, there's a lot to be gained!

Asking questions of other people demonstrates you are interested in them.
Think about how you feel when someone asks you:
'How are you getting on?' 'How's your work going?' 'How are your children?' 'How do you manage to be so good at painting?' 'How did you learn that?' Generally speaking we feel pretty good when people take an interest in us – so why don't we think others might feel the same way when we're the one's asking the questions? Becoming more interested in the lives of others is a sure-fire way of deepening relationship.

Asking questions is the easiest way to develop conversation.
Many people are shy and embarrassed in other people's company. They don't know what to say and conversation become stilted and mono-syllabled. Asking people questions is the best way out of this quagmire – people like to be asked and as already mentioned, we don't need to know anything at all before we start! Asking questions will help us overcome some of our awkwardness in social contexts, but only if we're willing to confront the barriers and become vulnerable – opening our mouth means we take a risk every time, but give it a go.

Asking questions tells someone you don't think you have all the answers. Unfortunately, as Christians, we have too often translated the fact of Jesus being the way, the truth and the life into arrogance, presumption and domination, none of which are worthy of the name of Jesus. We may well know Jesus is the way and the other person we are speaking with is walking in another direction, but simply telling them, without demonstrating we are walking with him, may easily leave them with an impression the followers of Jesus are just pushy and arrogant. Knowing Jesus is the truth sometimes comes across as suggesting people know nothing at all about truth and are 100% wrong in all their thinking. Unfortunately, we miss the log in our own eye by trying to point out the speck in others and they see us as presumptuous and dismissive. When we come across as those knowing we are 'saved', but everyone else is 'lost' with no sense of understanding or compassion of what it's like in their shoes, we begin to sound like a previous generation who confused the kingdom of God with the advance of nationalism. None of this expresses the life of Jesus in a way people are readily attracted by, which defeats what began as our primary concern. Asking people questions about their lives, faith and relationships tends to disarm people and actually helps them hear what eventually you have to say for yourself – in fact, more often than not, it provokes them to ask you themselves.

So, my suggestion is you begin taking note of what's going on in the conversations you are a part of and introduce, intentionally, more question asking into the equation and simply monitor the results, people's responses and your own. Asking questions implies we don't know all the answers and lets people know we are vulnerable people ourselves, not self-sufficient islands of omni-competence.

So asking questions of people is the practice, but only the means to building availability as a habit.

Jesus did not separate head and heart because he was 'full of grace and truth'. We find these all too easy to divide. It was, I suggest, part of Jesus' very nature to see no dividing line between the two. In this sense, created in the image of God, we (and everyone else we meet) are all like Jesus – that is we are not simply rational and intellectual human beings, but also emotional and relational ones to. One simple way to help avoid falling into the trap of dividing grace from truth with other people is to think more about what questions we might ask one another, in our DNA group, rather than what answers we shall prepare to offer. It is highly illuminating to simply note how many conversations Jesus himself began by asking a question – when, if anyone already knew the answer it was him! I tend to think this had something about his desire to start from where they were, rather than jump in from where he wanted them to arrive at. When you look at it like that, there's a world of difference between to two starting points, but then that's all wrapped up with the nature of God.

---

[i] Jacques Ellul (Geoffrey W Bromiley trans.) What I Believe (Grand Papids, Eerdmans, 1990) p54.

THE PASSAGE for this month: Luke 10:25-37 is this month's passage. Listen to the same passage, at least each week when you meet together, asking where, or what, God is calling for your attention. Mark down, in the weekly table on the next page, which facet (at least one) of the following three areas of your relationships God might be speaking into:

D for discipleship – our relationship with God.
N for engagement – our relationship with others.
A for authenticity – our relationship with ourselves.

MY PRAYER FOCUS: The three people I am going to pray for, each week, this month, are:	
1	
2	
3	

MY PRACTISING: Additionally, read the material on "availability" and consider what you might 'practice' to develop what it means to engage more meaningfully with others in your own life:

1. What do I need to practice this month?
It is important you decide clearly what you're going to actually do. For example, don't vaguely write 'read a book', specify which book and how much you'll read per week.

2. When do I intend to practice?
Precisely 'when'. Will it be daily, weekly, etc. If you're dependent upon opportunities arising, when will you notice them?

3. How can I ensure I do practice?
A note in your diary, a regular time in a certain place, something else needing to go to make space? Most people can't simply add more time consuming items into already too busy schedules. Do I share in my DNA group what I'm doing and ask them to ask me in x weeks time, do I put a note in the diary to ask myself? etc.

AVAILABILITY – week 1.   **LUKE 10:25-37.**

LOOK: Where in this passage is God calling for my attention?

In the light of this, what might God be saying to me in at least one facet of my life? Circle one, or more, facet of your relationships: D N A

LISTEN: What is God up to? (in my life, or those around me).

LIVE: Where have I seen God at work?

LEARN: What am I learning from my experience over the past week?

This week make sure you address this question:
'Where do I need more momentum?' in relation to 'following' Jesus this month:

ADDITIONAL NOTES ON THIS PASSAGE:

LOOK: Where in this passage is God calling for my attention?

In the light of this, what might God be saying to me in at least one facet of my life? Circle one, or more, facet of your relationships: D N A

LISTEN: What is God up to? (in my life, or those around me).

LIVE: Where have I seen God at work?

LEARN: What am I learning from my experience over the past week?

This week make sure you address this question:
What practices shall we try this month?

ADDITIONAL NOTES ON THIS PASSAGE:

AVAILABILITY – week 3.   **LUKE 10:25-37.**

LOOK: Where in this passage is God calling for my attention?

In the light of this, what might God be saying to me in at least one facet of my life? Circle one, or more, facet of your relationships: D N A

LISTEN: What is God up to? (in my life, or those around me).

LIVE: Where have I seen God at work?

LEARN: What am I learning from my experience over the past week?

This week make sure you address this question:
Who are we praying for?

ADDITIONAL NOTES ON THIS PASSAGE:

LOOK: Where in this passage is God calling for my attention?

In the light of this, what might God be saying to me in at least one facet of my life? Circle one, or more, facet of your relationships: D N A

LISTEN: What is God up to? (in my life, or those around me).

LIVE: Where have I seen God at work?

LEARN: What am I learning from my experience over the past week?

This week make sure you address this question:
How are we getting on with our practices?

ADDITIONAL NOTES ON THIS PASSAGE:

AVAILABILITY – week 5.

LOOK: Where, primarily over this month, in this passage is God calling for my attention?

In the light of this, what might God be saying to me in at least one facet of my life? Circle one, or more, facet of your relationships: D N A

LISTEN: What, in summary this month, is God up to? (in my life, or those around me).

LIVE: Where, pre-dominantly this month, have I seen God at work?

LEARN: What, mainly, am I learning from my experience over the past month?
Which have you circled most this month (D,N, or A)?

This week make sure you address this question:
How can we encourage one another with our practices?

ADDITIONAL NOTES ON THIS PASSAGE:

LOOK: Where in this passage is God calling for my attention?

In the light of this, what might God be saying to me in at least one facet of my life? Circle one, or more, facet of your relationships: D N A

LISTEN: What is God up to? (in my life, or those around me).

LIVE: Where have I seen God at work?

LEARN: What am I learning from my experience over the past week?

This week make sure you address this question:
'Where do I need more momentum?' in relation to 'following' Jesus this month:

ADDITIONAL NOTES ON THIS PASSAGE:

AUTHENTICITY – week 2.   **MATTHEW 5:1-16.**

LOOK: Where in this passage is God calling for my attention?

In the light of this, what might God be saying to me in at least one facet of my life? Circle one, or more, facet of your relationships: D N A

LISTEN: What is God up to? (in my life, or those around me).

LIVE: Where have I seen God at work?

LEARN: What am I learning from my experience over the past week?

This week make sure you address this question:
What practices shall we try this month?

ADDITIONAL NOTES ON THIS PASSAGE:

AUTHENTICITY – week 3.   MATTHEW 5:1-16.

LOOK: Where in this passage is God calling for my attention?

In the light of this, what might God be saying to me in at least one facet of my life? Circle one, or more, facet of your relationships: D N A

LISTEN: What is God up to? (in my life, or those around me).

LIVE: Where have I seen God at work?

LEARN: What am I learning from my experience over the past week?

This week make sure you address this question:
Who are we praying for?

ADDITIONAL NOTES ON THIS PASSAGE:

AUTHENTICITY – week 4. MATTHEW 5:1-16.

LOOK: Where in this passage is God calling for my attention?

In the light of this, what might God be saying to me in at least one facet of my life? Circle one, or more, facet of your relationships: D N A

LISTEN: What is God up to? (in my life, or those around me).

LIVE: Where have I seen God at work?

LEARN: What am I learning from my experience over the past week?

This week make sure you address this question:
How are we getting on with our practices?

ADDITIONAL NOTES ON THIS PASSAGE:

LOOK: Where, primarily over this month, in this passage is God calling for my attention?

In the light of this, what might God be saying to me in at least one facet of my life? Circle one, or more, facet of your relationships: D N A

LISTEN: What, in summary this month, is God up to? (in my life, or those around me).

LIVE: Where, pre-dominantly this month, have I seen God at work?

LEARN: What, mainly, am I learning from my experience over the past month?
Which have you circled most this month (D,N, or A)?

This week make sure you address this question:
How can we encourage one another with our practices?

ADDITIONAL NOTES ON THIS PASSAGE:

OPENNESS

…. from being seen through to being see-through.

If no one sees who you really are, how will they know what they really get?

'Change will not come if we wait for some other person or some other time. We are the ones we've been waiting for. We are the change that we seek.' Barack Obama. [i]

'If people really knew me, they wouldn't like what they see and wouldn't want to know me. It's much easier to pretend.' It may have simply been one individual in a counselling session, but I have subsequently observed and heard this represents the understanding of a huge number of people. Dare I suggest, all of us, to some degree? Superficiality, fuelled by the images constructed and imagined by consumerism and materialism, are at epidemic proportions.

'Come and see a man who told me all I ever did. Can this be the Christ?' [ii] Jesus reveals who he is, the woman concerned understands Jesus sees precisely who she is, inside-out, there's openness, transparency and vulnerability in abundance and it all begins with Jesus asking a question.

'We've only just met, but I feel as if we've known each other all our lives.'
'We don't see each other for years at a time, but we just pick up from where we left off as if we spend every day together.'
Some relationships just click. They might be romantically inclined, as in the first example, or simply the testimony of old friends, but that core idea of knowing someone well and being known by them is at the core of friendships, which go beneath the surface and last beyond the revelation of reality.

So, to what extent do other people see who you really are?
WYSIWYG, or 'what you see is what you get', was the buzz phrase when home computers took a leap forward a few years back, but it

doesn't seem to become the watchword for many people. What people see seems to be very rarely what they, or we, get.

Becoming authentic disciples of Jesus is clearly an all-embracing and life-long challenge for anyone. During our first month's focus upon 'authenticity', we focused upon the vital importance of maintaining a genuine relationship between the different aspects, which make up who we are – integrity. This month, our focus is upon 'openness' – the means by which we reveal who we actually are. Be warned, it will be a challenge. However, think about what it means to know someone who we feel demonstrates openness. They are a delight to be with, we feel they are accepting of us, we feel we dare share anything about ourselves, we do not feel condemned, but we might feel challenged. Openness is one of those aspects of character, which has a magnetic quality about it. Another word, far less attractive, is 'vulnerability'. There's a massive overlap between these two ideas and there is no doubt openness, concerning who we truly are, with other people leaves us feeling very vulnerable at times.

Every beatitude Jesus introduces at the beginning of the sermon of the mount (this month's focus passage) is itself a challenge. [iii] Many have seen a progression from one to the other, but they are all exemplified and seen most clearly in Jesus himself. Undoubtedly, there are aspects to the person of Jesus Christ, which are not obvious and shrouded in a degree of mystery he seems to almost cultivate. However, whilst this might apply to dimensions of his identity and mission, it is never the case about his character. What you see in Jesus is what you get. The words you hear from the mouth of Jesus are always the overflow of a heart 100% in tune with his Father, our God. Developing an openness of character towards others, to the point it becomes habitually part of who we are demands, however, we know ourselves. Do we know who we really are? Self-awareness, or a growing self-awareness, is something everyone of us will undoubtedly benefit from. One of the chief reasons most of us get stuck with growing in self-awareness is the lack of genuine friendships where we can be honest and open, but accepted and loved. Every DNA group has the potential to become such an environment, but it takes time and it takes courage by all.

Where does openness and wearing your heart on your sleeve differ? It seems clear to most people that telling everyone everything about yourself is a recipe for disaster, whereas being a closed book and never revealing anything tends towards pulling up the drawbridge for genuine friendship to take place.

Have a look at this table and think through where you are on this spectrum and where giving some more attention might reap the greatest benefits.

Appropriate self-disclosure	Inappropriate self-disclosure
Respecting your own self-definition.	Unable to differentiate between your wants and needs.
Asserting your wants and wishes.	Disregarding others.
Owning your feelings and emotions.	Overwhelmed by your feelings and emotions.
Expressing liking and being likeable.	Lacking integrity and simply telling people what they want.
Able to reveal both strengths and weaknesses.	Disrespecting boundaries.

Openness brings vulnerability, but vulnerability often brings fear – fear of rejection. Here's a very brief summary of where Jesus demonstrates his willingness to be vulnerable, but it would be much better for you to check the gospels out for yourself:

In birth.
In childhood.
In calling disciples.
In his own district.
In meeting individuals.
In challenging authorities.
In attending inappropriate gatherings.
In presenting teaching.
In revealing the truth of God.
In identifying with the poor, the marginalised, the defenceless.
In answering his accusers.
In not defending himself.
In death.
In commissioning disciples.

In a world where people are wanting to sit down and debate the truth of an argument, or where a decision to follow Jesus rests on an academic case for the existence of God, or his creation of the world, then you don't look for develop vulnerability. Show them your argument has vulnerabilities, is not fully and carefully thought through then you'll risk losing the argument and the potential believer. It's an approach where all you need is your head, but it's an approach, which I have found doesn't grow much fruit.

In a world where people are suspicious of anyone who claims to have some authority, the decision to follow Jesus, or not, will have little to do with whether your truth is better than theirs. Allow someone to see your vulnerabilities, uncertainties and doubts. Alongside this let them can see another person dealing with the same realities of things they will know as much about for themselves, but someone who is able to live a life of faith and trust. What happens? You might lose an argument or two, but gain a friend who has a heart as well as a head. Who knows, they might even decide to give Jesus a hearing too! Of course, whilst we're looking at developing a habit of being open to others under the 'authenticity/loving others as ourselves' heading, it is clearly related to developing our relationship with God and our neighbour also.

' When I got to know Fran there was something different about her, I just had to find out for myself.'

'I could see this was a group of friends who had something special I didn't have.'

'I came to respect Mike for his honesty and integrity. I now know what made him different was Jesus.'

All these are simple testimonies from baptismal services. The truth is people respond to people like them, relationships where they sense another dimension, a missing piece, whatever they start to call it, but it's the reality of Jesus. 'No one lights a lamp and shoves it under the bed.' [iv]

Before you leap head first into a new commitment to becoming more vulnerable, here's some words, which summarise the responses to Jesus' willingness in this area:

People's reaction.	Jesus' response.	My reaction?
Life-threatening	'my kingdom is not of this world'. [v]	
Rejection	'he who rejects me, rejects the one who sent me' [vi]	
Ridicule	Silence – upon the cross [vii]	
Mis-understanding	'you have said so' [viii]	
False accusation	Silence – before Pilate.	
Desertion & disowning.	'do you love me?' - a question towards restoration. [ix]	
Death	'father forgive them for they do not know what they are doing' [x]	

The truth is any relationship, which goes beyond the traditional ....
'Hello, how are you?' .... 'I'm fine thanks, are you?' .... 'Yes, fine.'
'OK, see you soon. Bye' .... is bound to make us vulnerable because we'll become known for who we really are, rather than who we like to suggest to people we're like.

One practice we could use to develop openness is the idea of keeping short accounts. How good are you? Be honest!
Practicing keeping short accounts with God and others does not invariably involve telling anyone what they do not already see in us, but it does convey a willingness to change, admit we're not the centre of the universe and they have an important place too. It does require discipline.
Practice check-list before you go to sleep each night:

Is there anything I need to confess to God?
Is there anyone I need to say 'sorry' to?
Is there anyone I need to forgive?
Whatever the answer decide, there and then, when you'll act

[i] Barack Obama in a recorded speech 5th. February, 2011.
[ii] John 4:29.

[iii] Matthew, chapters 5-7, are generally recognized as ;the sermon on the mount'.
[iv] Luke 8:16.
[v] John 18:36.
[vi] Luke 10:15-17.
[vii] Luke 23:35-43.
[viii] Matthew 27:11.
[ix] John 21:15-25.
[x] Luke 23:35

THE PASSAGE for this month: Matthew 6: 5-24 is this month's passage. Listen to the same passage, at least each week when you meet together, asking where, or what, God is calling for your attention. Mark down, in the weekly table on the next page, which facet (at least one) of the following three areas of your relationships God might be speaking into:

D for discipleship – our relationship with God.
N for engagement – our relationship with others.
A for authenticity – our relationship with ourselves.

MY PRAYER FOCUS: The three people I am going to pray for, each week, this month, are:	
1	
2	
3	

MY PRACTISING: Additionally, read the material on "openess" and consider what you might 'practice' to develop what it means to engage more meaningfully with others in your own life:

1. What do I need to practice this month?
It is important you decide clearly what you're going to actually do. For example, don't vaguely write 'read a book', specify which book and how much you'll read per week.

2. When do I intend to practice?
Precisely 'when'. Will it be daily, weekly, etc. If you're dependent upon opportunities arising, when will you notice them?

3. How can I ensure I do practice?
A note in your diary, a regular time in a certain place, something else needing to go to make space? Most people can't simply add more time consuming items into already too busy schedules. Do I share in my DNA group what I'm doing and ask them to ask me in x weeks time, do I put a note in the diary to ask myself? etc.

OPENNESS - week 1.   **MATTHEW 6:5-24.**

LOOK: Where in this passage is God calling for my attention?

In the light of this, what might God be saying to me in at least one facet of my life? Circle one, or more, facet of your relationships: D N A

LISTEN: What is God up to? (in my life, or those around me).

LIVE: Where have I seen God at work?

LEARN: What am I learning from my experience over the past week?

This week make sure you address this question:
'Where do I need more momentum?' in relation to 'following' Jesus this month:

ADDITIONAL NOTES ON THIS PASSAGE:

LOOK:　　　Where in this passage is God calling for my attention?

In the light of this, what might God be saying to me in at least one facet of my life? Circle one, or more, facet of your relationships: D N A

LISTEN:　　What is God up to? (in my life, or those around me).

LIVE:　　　Where have I seen God at work?

LEARN:　　What am I learning from my experience over the past week?

This week make sure you address this question:
What practices shall we try this month?

ADDITIONAL NOTES ON THIS PASSAGE:

LOOK: Where in this passage is God calling for my attention?

In the light of this, what might God be saying to me in at least one facet of my life? Circle one, or more, facet of your relationships: D N A

LISTEN: What is God up to? (in my life, or those around me).

LIVE: Where have I seen God at work?

LEARN: What am I learning from my experience over the past week?

This week make sure you address this question:
Who are we praying for?

ADDITIONAL NOTES ON THIS PASSAGE:

OPENNESS – **week 4.**   **MATTHEW 6:5-24.**

LOOK: Where in this passage is God calling for my attention?

In the light of this, what might God be saying to me in at least one facet
of my life? Circle one, or more, facet of your relationships: D N A

LISTEN: What is God up to? (in my life, or those around me).

LIVE: Where have I seen God at work?

LEARN: What am I learning from my experience over the past week?

This week make sure you address this question:
How are we getting on with our practices?

ADDITIONAL NOTES ON THIS PASSAGE:

LOOK: Where, primarily over this month, in this passage is God calling for my attention?

In the light of this, what might God be saying to me in at least one facet of my life? Circle one, or more, facet of your relationships: D N A

LISTEN: What, in summary this month, is God up to? (in my life, or those around me).

LIVE: Where, pre-dominantly this month, have I seen God at work?

LEARN: What, mainly, am I learning from my experience over the past month?
Which have you circled most this month (D,N, or A)?

This week make sure you address this question:
How can we encourage one another with our practices?

ADDITIONAL NOTES ON THIS PASSAGE:

AUTHENTICITY – week 1.   MATTHEW 5:1-16.

LOOK: Where in this passage is God calling for my attention?

In the light of this, what might God be saying to me in at least one facet of my life? Circle one, or more, facet of your relationships: D N A

LISTEN: What is God up to? (in my life, or those around me).

LIVE: Where have I seen God at work?

LEARN: What am I learning from my experience over the past week?

This week make sure you address this question:
'Where do I need more momentum?' in relation to 'following' Jesus this month:

ADDITIONAL NOTES ON THIS PASSAGE:

AUTHENTICITY – week 2.   **MATTHEW 5:1-16.**

LOOK: Where in this passage is God calling for my attention?

In the light of this, what might God be saying to me in at least one facet of my life? Circle one, or more, facet of your relationships: D N A

LISTEN: What is God up to? (in my life, or those around me).

LIVE: Where have I seen God at work?

LEARN: What am I learning from my experience over the past week?

This week make sure you address this question:
What practices shall we try this month?

ADDITIONAL NOTES ON THIS PASSAGE:

LOOK: Where in this passage is God calling for my attention?

In the light of this, what might God be saying to me in at least one facet of my life? Circle one, or more, facet of your relationships: D N A

LISTEN: What is God up to? (in my life, or those around me).

LIVE: Where have I seen God at work?

LEARN: What am I learning from my experience over the past week?

This week make sure you address this question:
Who are we praying for?

ADDITIONAL NOTES ON THIS PASSAGE:

AUTHENTICITY – week 4.   **MATTHEW 5:1-16.**

LOOK: Where in this passage is God calling for my attention?

In the light of this, what might God be saying to me in at least one facet of my life? Circle one, or more, facet of your relationships: D N A

LISTEN: What is God up to? (in my life, or those around me).

LIVE: Where have I seen God at work?

LEARN: What am I learning from my experience over the past week?

This week make sure you address this question:
How are we getting on with our practices?

ADDITIONAL NOTES ON THIS PASSAGE:

LOOK: Where, primarily over this month, in this passage is God calling for my attention?

In the light of this, what might God be saying to me in at least one facet of my life? Circle one, or more, facet of your relationships: D N A

LISTEN: What, in summary this month, is God up to? (in my life, or those around me).

LIVE: Where, pre-dominantly this month, have I seen God at work?

LEARN: What, mainly, am I learning from my experience over the past month?
Which have you circled most this month (D,N, or A)?

This week make sure you address this question:
How can we encourage one another with our practices?

ADDITIONAL NOTES ON THIS PASSAGE:

BELOVING.

.... from superficiality to love of another kind.

'To love another person is to help them love God'. Soren Kierkegaard.

'Let your religion be less of a theory and more of a love affair'. GK Chesterton.

To unpack the discipleship strand of Christian DNA, so far, we've looked at 'following' (month one) and 'learning' (month four) because they are the two, which seem to best describe, the meaning of the actual word. 'Beloving' is our next focus word to unpack what it means to be a disciple of Jesus. Love, as widely recognised, is probably the most overused word in the English language. Unfortunately, it may the most under practised too. We cannot, however, avoid love's challenge. When asked to give an answer to name the most important commandment, Jesus goes for 'love':

'The most important one,' answered Jesus, is this: 'Hear O Israel: the Lord our God, the Lord is one. *Love* the Lord your God with all your heart and with all your soul and with all your mind and with all your strength'. The second is this: '*Love* your neighbour as yourself'. There is no commandment greater than these'. [i] Jesus highlights the three strands of Christian DNA, but attributes 'love' to them all.

So, when asked for one answer, why did Jesus give two? We are talking about the whole of life, one life, but our life, as God intended it. Love remains the word above all others, which both sums up and also embraces the breadth of what living out the life of Jesus is ultimately about. However, even our loving of God can only be fully expressed in loving 'one another' (in the kingdom of God), loving 'our neighbour' and loving ourselves.

Some of the saddest conversations I have been included in have been those between a couple struggling to fan into life the dying embers of their relationship. One thing, which makes them so tragic, is the almost hypnotic regularity of the conversation. Different couples, same words:

He says: 'Of course I love you.' She says: 'but you never say so.'
She says: 'Of course I love you.' He says: 'but you never show me.'

If the love of God is not being seen in you, where has it gone? It is insufficient for anyone to have to assume you love if you remain silent. Equally, it is insufficient for anyone to assume you love if there is no evidence. Words and action belong together and nowhere more necessary than in a relationship where love is the glue, which stuck them together. So, my challenge to any would-be disciple of Jesus: before you set about changing the world, is to ensure those whom God has already given you never need to ask the question Jesus found it necessary to ask Peter - 'do you love me?'

It is more of a surprise to me us Brits only have one word 'love', whereas others, the Greeks for example, require five:

Phileo – regard with affection, as with a friend.
Agape – unconditional love, even given to enemies.
Stergo – affectionate love as with parents towards children.
Eros – passionate love, with sensual desire or longing.
Hetaireia – companionship, sharing common concerns, or issues.

It may be we need to evaluate, which dimension of love we need to appropriately express, in any given situation. However, we are left in no doubt that, for the follower of Jesus, love is not an option.

Take some time to listen to some of the words of Jesus concerning love:

'I tell you, love your enemies'. [ii]
'If you love those who love you, what reward will you get?' [iii]
'To love Him with all your heart, and with all your understanding and with all your strength, and to love your neighbour as yourself is more important than all burnt offerings or sacrifices'. [iv]
'Even sinners love those who love them'. [v]
'Love one another, as I have loved you'. [vi]
'If you love me, you will obey what I command'. [vii]
'Greater love has no one than this: to lay his life for his friends'. [viii]

I would recommend you study them all by using a concordance and see what you notice. What strikes me is how practical Jesus makes it all. Time and time again he roots what love is in practical examples. He binds it to real life. Nowhere does Jesus paint love as a concept devoid of real practical expression.

So, this month, I'm asking you to focus upon practising sacrificial love. I'm calling for an application of agape love – the unconditional love of another kind, which Jesus has introduced into our vocabulary. What that looks like and how it is expressed, will be as varied as the relationships you choose to focus it on. All I suggest you do, is select an individual and then ask yourself 'what will love look like for them, if I decide to walk the second mile this week?' Read the passage about the vine and the branches again and this time, try and keep the person you are thinking about in mind. With each phrase Jesus speaks, ask how you might apply his words for them?

Sacrificial love costs. It may be our time, our money, or our energy, but there must be no pretending: genuine love is a costly experience. The fact is, we are being asked to love others as God loves us. 'God so loved the world that he gave his only Son, that whoever believes in him should not perish but have eternal life.' [ix] The most famous verse, I imagine, in the whole Bible. Believing God loves us unconditionally is a huge challenge for so many people, often because their experience of unconditional love from other human beings is all but non-existent. Every act of Christian love, in such a context, is a subversive blow against the enemy of the things of God. People do not expect, or believe they deserve, love which is not tied. Little in today's predominant culture prepares people for the surprise of unconditional love, but there's little doubt in my mind, it is the greatest visual aid to prepare anybody's heart for the heart of God. Real love, be warned, is not easy – you may give, but get nothing back.

Before I totally fall into the trap of trying too hard to explain the unexplainable, let me pass on one of my favourite stories – Sawat's story. [x]

He had disgraced his family and dishounoured his father's name. He has come to Bangkok to escape the dullness of village life. He had found excitement and while he prospered in his sordid lifestyle, he found popularity as well. When he first arrived, he had visited a hotel unlike any hotel he'd ever seen before. In each of the hotel rooms were teenage girls. Some as young as twelve years old and younger. Some of the girls were laughing and some looked nervous and scared.

That visit began Sawat's adventure into Bangkok's world of prostitution. It began innocently enough, but he was quickly caught like a small piece of wood in a raging river. It's force was too powerful and swift for him, the current too strong. Soon he selling opium to customers and propositioning tourists in the hotels. He even went so low as to actually help buy and sell young girls, some of them only none and ten years old. It was a nasty business and he was one of the most important of the young 'businessmen'.

Then the bottom dropped out of Sawat's world: he hit a string of bad luck. He was robbed and while trying to climb back to the top, he was arrested. The word went out in the underworld he was a police spy. He finally ended up living in a shanty by the city trash pile. Sitting in his little shack, he thought about his family, especially his father, a simple Christian man from a small southern village near the Malaysian border. He remembered his dad's parting words: 'I am waiting for you.' He wondered whether his father would still be waiting for him after all that he had done to dishonour the family name. Would he be welcome in his home? Word of Sawat's lifestyle had long ago filtered back to the village.

Finally he devised a plan.

'Dear Father,' he wrote. 'I wanted to come home, but I don't know if you will receive me after all I have done. I have sinned greatly, father. Please forgive me. On Saturday night I will be on the train that goes through our village. If you are still waiting for me, will you tie a piece of cloth on the Po tree in front of our house? (Signed) Sawat.

On that train ride he reflected on his life over the past few months and knew his father had very right to deny him. As the train finally neared the village, he churned with anxiety. What would he do if there was no cloth on the Po tree?

Sitting opposite him was a kind stranger who noticed how nervous his fellow passenger had become. Finally, Sawat could stand the pressure no more. He blurted out his story in a torrent of words. As they entered the village, Sawat said, 'Oh Sir, I cannot bear to look. Can you watch for me? What if my father will not receive me back?'

Sawat buried his face between his knees. 'Do you see it, Sir? It's the only house with a Po tree.'

'Young man, your father did not hang just one piece of cloth. Look! He has covered the whole tree with cloth!' Sawat could hardly believe his eyes. The branches were laden with tiny white squares of cloth. In the front yard his father jumped up and down, joyously waving a piece of white cloth, then ran in halting steps beside the train. When it stopped at the little station he threw his arms around his son, embracing him with tears of joy. 'I've been waiting for you!' he exclaimed.

You may well recognise the story of the Prodigal Son, which more accurately should be called the Waiting Father.

It may well be, the biggest blockage to us expressing the love of God to fellow human beings, is our inability, or unwillingness, to receive the love of God for ourselves. Maybe you need to stop right now and ask whether you need to ask God to fill you again with his love. One of the biggest mistakes we make as followers of Jesus, is when we assume we must provide what we need to give to others, simply from our own resources. Speaking for myself, I ran out of those on day one. The good news is God supplies fresh grace every day.

---

[i] Mark 12:29-31.
[ii] Matthew 5:44.
[iii] Matthew 5:46.
[iv] Mark 12: 33.
[v] Luke 6:32.
[vi] John 13:34.
[vii] John 14:15.
[viii] John 15:13.
[ix] John 3:16.
[x] The Father Heart of God, Floyd McClung.

THE PASSAGE for this month: Matthew 6: 5-24 is this month's passage. Listen to the same passage, at least each week when you meet together, asking where, or what, God is calling for your attention. Mark down, in the weekly table on the next page, which facet (at least one) of the following three areas of your relationships God might be speaking into:

D for discipleship – our relationship with God.
N for engagement – our relationship with others.
A for authenticity – our relationship with ourselves.

MY PRAYER FOCUS: The three people I am going to pray for, each week, this month, are:	
1	
2	
3	

MY PRACTISING: Additionally, read the material on "beloving" and consider what you might 'practice' to develop what it means to engage more meaningfully with others in your own life:

1. What do I need to practice this month?
It is important you decide clearly what you're going to actually do. For example, don't vaguely write 'read a book', specify which book and how much you'll read per week.

2. When do I intend to practice?
Precisely 'when'. Will it be daily, weekly, etc. If you're dependent upon opportunities arising, when will you notice them?

3. How can I ensure I do practice?
A note in your diary, a regular time in a certain place, something else needing to go to make space? Most people can't simply add more time consuming items into already too busy schedules. Do I share in my DNA group what I'm doing and ask them to ask me in x weeks time, do I put a note in the diary to ask myself? etc.

LOOK: Where in this passage is God calling for my attention?

In the light of this, what might God be saying to me in at least one facet of my life? Circle one, or more, facet of your relationships: D N A

LISTEN: What is God up to? (in my life, or those around me).

LIVE: Where have I seen God at work?

LEARN: What am I learning from my experience over the past week?

This week make sure you address this question:
'Where do I need more momentum?' in relation to 'following' Jesus this month:

ADDITIONAL NOTES ON THIS PASSAGE:

BELOVING – week 2.   **JOHN 15; 1-17.**

LOOK: Where in this passage is God calling for my attention?

In the light of this, what might God be saying to me in at least one facet of my life? Circle one, or more, facet of your relationships: D N A

LISTEN: What is God up to? (in my life, or those around me).

LIVE: Where have I seen God at work?

LEARN: What am I learning from my experience over the past week?

This week make sure you address this question:
What practices shall we try this month?

ADDITIONAL NOTES ON THIS PASSAGE:

LOOK: Where in this passage is God calling for my attention?

In the light of this, what might God be saying to me in at least one facet of my life? Circle one, or more, facet of your relationships: D N A

LISTEN: What is God up to? (in my life, or those around me).

LIVE: Where have I seen God at work?

LEARN: What am I learning from my experience over the past week?

This week make sure you address this question:
Who are we praying for?

ADDITIONAL NOTES ON THIS PASSAGE:

BELOVING – week 4.   JOHN 15; 1-17.

LOOK: Where in this passage is God calling for my attention?

In the light of this, what might God be saying to me in at least one facet of my life? Circle one, or more, facet of your relationships: D N A

LISTEN: What is God up to? (in my life, or those around me).

LIVE: Where have I seen God at work?

LEARN: What am I learning from my experience over the past week?

This week make sure you address this question:
How are we getting on with our practices?

ADDITIONAL NOTES ON THIS PASSAGE:

LOOK: Where, primarily over this month, in this passage is God calling for my attention?

In the light of this, what might God be saying to me in at least one facet of my life? Circle one, or more, facet of your relationships: D N A

LISTEN: What, in summary this month, is God up to? (in my life, or those around me).

LIVE: Where, pre-dominantly this month, have I seen God at work?

LEARN: What, mainly, am I learning from my experience over the past month?
Which have you circled most this month (D,N, or A)?

This week make sure you address this question:
How can we encourage one another with our practices?

ADDITIONAL NOTES ON THIS PASSAGE:

LOOK: Where in this passage is God calling for my attention?

In the light of this, what might God be saying to me in at least one facet of my life? Circle one, or more, facet of your relationships: D N A

LISTEN: What is God up to? (in my life, or those around me).

LIVE: Where have I seen God at work?

LEARN: What am I learning from my experience over the past week?

This week make sure you address this question:
'Where do I need more momentum?' in relation to 'following' Jesus this month:

ADDITIONAL NOTES ON THIS PASSAGE:

AUTHENTICITY - week 2.   MATTHEW 5:1-16.

LOOK: Where in this passage is God calling for my attention?

In the light of this, what might God be saying to me in at least one facet
of my life? Circle one, or more, facet of your relationships: D N A

LISTEN: What is God up to? (in my life, or those around me).

LIVE: Where have I seen God at work?

LEARN: What am I learning from my experience over the past week?

This week make sure you address this question:
What practices shall we try this month?

ADDITIONAL NOTES ON THIS PASSAGE:

AUTHENTICITY – week 3.   **MATTHEW 5:1-16.**

LOOK: Where in this passage is God calling for my attention?

In the light of this, what might God be saying to me in at least one facet of my life? Circle one, or more, facet of your relationships: D N A

LISTEN: What is God up to? (in my life, or those around me).

LIVE: Where have I seen God at work?

LEARN: What am I learning from my experience over the past week?

This week make sure you address this question:
Who are we praying for?

ADDITIONAL NOTES ON THIS PASSAGE:

AUTHENTICITY – week 4.   **MATTHEW 5:1-16.**

LOOK: Where in this passage is God calling for my attention?

In the light of this, what might God be saying to me in at least one facet of my life? Circle one, or more, facet of your relationships: D N A

LISTEN: What is God up to? (in my life, or those around me).

LIVE: Where have I seen God at work?

LEARN: What am I learning from my experience over the past week?

This week make sure you address this question:
How are we getting on with our practices?

ADDITIONAL NOTES ON THIS PASSAGE:

AUTHENTICITY - week 5.

LOOK: Where, primarily over this month, in this passage is God calling for my attention?

In the light of this, what might God be saying to me in at least one facet of my life? Circle one, or more, facet of your relationships: D N A

LISTEN: What, in summary this month, is God up to? (in my life, or those around me).

LIVE: Where, pre-dominantly this month, have I seen God at work?

LEARN: What, mainly, am I learning from my experience over the past month?
Which have you circled most this month (D,N, or A)?

This week make sure you address this question:
How can we encourage one another with our practices?

ADDITIONAL NOTES ON THIS PASSAGE:

COMPASSION.

…. from being to doing.

'If you judge people, you have no time to love them'. Mother Teresa.

'Let no one ever come to you without leaving better and happier. Be the living expression of God's kindness: kindness I your face, kindness in your eyes, kindness in your smile'. Mother Teresa. [i]

Compassion is the human face of the servants of God.
You will influence at least 10,000 people before you die!
Sociologists tell us that even the most introverted individual will influence 10,000 other people during his, or her, lifetime. When I first heard this, it sounded a little far-fetched, but once you stop and start thinking about it, it becomes fairly obvious. Schoolmates, friends, teachers, work-colleagues, customers, family, etc. etc. They soon add up and who cares, if it's give or take a thousand or two - it's a lot of people!

We may get to the place where we accept the fact we all influence other people. However, the deeper question is, 'what kind of influence are we?' For good or evil, God or otherwise, light, or darkness? In a day and age where distinctions between such categories are un-comfortable for many people, as followers of Jesus we must face the question whether any relationship is ever purely neutral in its influence. For a Christian, this boils down to whether we're are an influence for God and for good in any relationship, or set of circumstances, or not? When we take a closer look at Jesus it's clear he had some kind of impact upon everyone he met. We do need to note carefully, however, he certainly didn't find the same response from them all.

Each September, Miss Thompson greeted the new children in her class with the words 'Boys and girls, I love you all the same. I have no favourites.' Of course, she wasn't entirely honest with herself, because teachers often do have favourites and what is worse, they sometimes have children they don't like.
Teddy Stallard as a boy Miss Thompson just didn't like, and for good reason. He was a sullen boy who sat slouched in his seat with is head

down. When she spoke to him he always answered in mono-syllables of "yes" and "no." His clothes were musty and his hair unkempt. He was an unattractive boy in just about every way. Whenever she marked Teddy's work she got aperverse delight out of putting X's next to the wrong answers and whenever she put an "F" at the top of his papers, she always did it with a flair. She should have known better. Teachers have records, and she had records on Teddy:

First grade: Teddy shows promise with is work and attitude, but poor home situation.
Second grade: Teddy is a good boy, but he is too serious for a second grader. His mother is terminally ill.
Third grade: Teddy is becoming withdrawn and detached. His mother died this year. His father shows no interest.
Fourth grade: Teddy is a troubled child. He needs help.

Christmas came. The children brought presents to Miss Thompson and piled them on her desk. They crowded around to watch her open them. All the presents were wrapped in brightly coloured paper, except for Teddy's present. His was wrapped in brown paper and held together with Scotch tape. But to tell you the truth, she was surprised he even bought her a present.
When she tore open the paper, out fell a rhinestone bracelet with most of the stones missing and an almost-empty bottle of cheap perfume. The other children giggled at the shabby gifts, but Miss Thompson had enough sense to snap on the bracelet and take some of the perfume and put it on her wrist. Holding her wrist up to the other children, she said, :Isn't it lovely?" The other children, taking their cue from their teacher, all agreed.
At the end of the day when all the children had left, Teddy came over to her desk and said softly, "Miss Thompson … all day today you smelled just like my mother used to smell. That's her bracelet you're wearing. It looks nice on you … I'm really glad you like my presents."
After he left, she got down on her knees and buried her head in her hands and cried and cried and cried, and she asked God to forgive her.
The next day when the children came to her class, they had a new teacher. It was till Miss Thompson, but she was a new teacher. She cared in ways that the old teacher didn't. She reached out to all the children, but especially to Teddy. She nurtured them and encouraged

them and tutored them when they needed extra help. By the end of that school year Teddy had caught up with a lot of children. He was even ahead of some.

Teddy moved away and Miss Thompson didn't hear from him for a long tme. Then one day, seemingly out of nowhere came a note:

Dear Miss Thompson,
I'm graduating from high school. I wanted you to be the first to know.
Love,
Teddy Stallard.

There was no address, but four years later there was another short note, and it read:

Dear Miss Thompson,
I wanted you to be the first to know. I'm second in my class. The University has not been easy, but I really liked it.
Love,
Teddy Stallard.

Then, four more years later, there was another note:

Dear Miss Thompson,
As of today I am Theodore J. Stallard, MD! How about that! I wanted you to be the first to know. I'm going to be married, the 27th. of July to be exact. I want you to come and I want you to sit where my mother would have sat. You're the only family I have now. Dad died last year.
Love,
Teddy Stallard.

Miss Thompson went and she sat where Teddy's mother would have sat ..... because she deserved to be there. Here is a teacher who has done something great for the Kingdom of God, and she deserved her reward. [ii] If compassion has a human face then why not yours?

Humility is the lens, through which compassion sees other people. Augustine wrote: "If you ask me what is the first precept of the Christian religion, I will answer first, second and third, humility". [iii] Humility is something we hardly dare suggest we might have, for fear our very suggestion will destroy the evidence. "If anyone would like to acquire humility, I can, I think, tell him the first step. The first step is to realise that one is proud. And a biggish step, too. At least, nothing can be done before it. If you think you are not conceited, it means you are very conceited indeed." [iv] My feeling is humility is something best encouraged by action, rather than anything else. We might wish to pray 'Lord, help me to have humility', but humility is like swimming – you can only really learn by jumping in. Finding excuses to act, as a means of blessing other people, is the real process, which encourages a growth of humility within us.

Whenever the subject of 'leadership' arises, the two sides of the debate soon emerge: are leaders born, or can they be made? When, however, the results of leadership are examined, one of the simplest, but best definitions is, 'leadership is influence'. That's where it's effects are seen. However, if leadership is influence, then influencing grows best when rooted in compassion. Think about it, who are your heroes, who do you admire most? I can almost guarantee the leaders you pick out will have their influence rooted in compassion (probably humility is the root!). Mother Teresa is one of the most influential leaders of the last century, yet she possessed nothing materially speaking. What she did possess, however, was humility seen in compassion.

If we cannot start by communicating respect for others, made in the image of God, maybe we need to start again. Acceptance of others, especially when they're different to us, is always a challenge. However, the Bible's call 'accept one another', means the community of God must rise to it.

If compassion is never seen in what we do, it was probably never truly there. Compassion un-practised is meaningless. There is no doubt, one of the biggest influences, helping my decision to write this tool-book, was hearing about some of things Michael Frost was encouraging in their fellowship 'Small boat, big sea.' [v] They use the acronym 'BELLS' to encourage one another to live by a simple rhythm – to regularly BLESS people (B), EAT with people (E), LISTEN to God (L), LEARN from God (L), and to see their life vocation as being SENT by God (S).

The Hebrew for blessing (barak) means "to empower to strength". Pass it on, must become the by-word for Christians, when to comes to the blessing of God, if we are to more clearly reflect the life of Jesus. Blessing others was clearly a habit of Jesus, so why not ours? In small boat, big sea they ask the weekly question 'who have you blessed this week through words, or actions and what learning, encouragement, or concerns were raised by it? I would love to think every Christian might reflect weekly on such a question. I realise the likelihood of this, or any of the other practices we raise each month, becoming a habit after one month, is naïve, but it may just get us started. So, let's make sure we start this week.

---

[i] Mother Teresa, reported quotes.
[ii] Tony Campolo, *Let me Tell You a Story*, Word Publishing. 2000. p.167.
[iii]

[iv] CS Lewis
[v] www.smallboatbigsea.org

THE PASSAGE for this month: Mark 6: 30-44 is this month's passage. Listen to the same passage, at least each week when you meet together, asking where, or what, God is calling for your attention. Mark down, in the weekly table on the next page, which facet (at least one) of the following three areas of your relationships God might be speaking into:

D for discipleship – our relationship with God.
N for engagement – our relationship with others.
A for authenticity – our relationship with ourselves.

MY PRAYER FOCUS: The three people I am going to pray for, each week, this month, are:	
1	
2	
3	

MY PRACTISING: Additionally, read the material on "compassion" and consider what you might 'practice' to develop what it means to engage more meaningfully with others in your own life:

1. What do I need to practice this month?
It is important you decide clearly what you're going to actually do. For example, don't vaguely write 'read a book', specify which book and how much you'll read per week.

2. When do I intend to practice?
Precisely 'when'. Will it be daily, weekly, etc. If you're dependent upon opportunities arising, when will you notice them?

3. How can I ensure I do practice?
A note in your diary, a regular time in a certain place, something else needing to go to make space? Most people can't simply add more time consuming items into already too busy schedules. Do I share in my DNA group what I'm doing and ask them to ask me in x weeks time, do I put a note in the diary to ask myself? etc.

COMPASSION – week 1. MARK 6; 30-44.

LOOK: Where in this passage is God calling for my attention?

In the light of this, what might God be saying to me in at least one facet of my life? Circle one, or more, facet of your relationships: D N A

LISTEN: What is God up to? (in my life, or those around me).

LIVE: Where have I seen God at work?

LEARN: What am I learning from my experience over the past week?

This week make sure you address this question:
'Where do I need more momentum?' in relation to 'following' Jesus this month:

ADDITIONAL NOTES ON THIS PASSAGE:

COMPASSION – week 2.

LOOK: Where in this passage is God calling for my attention?

In the light of this, what might God be saying to me in at least one facet of my life? Circle one, or more, facet of your relationships: D N A

LISTEN: What is God up to? (in my life, or those around me).

LIVE: Where have I seen God at work?

LEARN: What am I learning from my experience over the past week?

This week make sure you address this question:
What practices shall we try this month?

ADDITIONAL NOTES ON THIS PASSAGE:

LOOK: Where in this passage is God calling for my attention?

In the light of this, what might God be saying to me in at least one facet of my life? Circle one, or more, facet of your relationships: D N A

LISTEN: What is God up to? (in my life, or those around me).

LIVE: Where have I seen God at work?

LEARN: What am I learning from my experience over the past week?

This week make sure you address this question:
Who are we praying for?

ADDITIONAL NOTES ON THIS PASSAGE:

COMPASSION – week 4.

LOOK: Where in this passage is God calling for my attention?

In the light of this, what might God be saying to me in at least one facet of my life? Circle one, or more, facet of your relationships: D N A

LISTEN: What is God up to? (in my life, or those around me).

LIVE: Where have I seen God at work?

LEARN: What am I learning from my experience over the past week?

This week make sure you address this question:
How are we getting on with our practices?

ADDITIONAL NOTES ON THIS PASSAGE:

LOOK: Where, primarily over this month, in this passage is God calling for my attention?

In the light of this, what might God be saying to me in at least one facet of my life? Circle one, or more, facet of your relationships: D N A

LISTEN: What, in summary this month, is God up to? (in my life, or those around me).

LIVE: Where, pre-dominantly this month, have I seen God at work?

LEARN: What, mainly, am I learning from my experience over the past month?
Which have you circled most this month (D,N, or A)?

This week make sure you address this question:
How can we encourage one another with our practices?

ADDITIONAL NOTES ON THIS PASSAGE:

LOOK: Where in this passage is God calling for my attention?

In the light of this, what might God be saying to me in at least one facet of my life? Circle one, or more, facet of your relationships: D N A

LISTEN: What is God up to? (in my life, or those around me).

LIVE: Where have I seen God at work?

LEARN: What am I learning from my experience over the past week?

This week make sure you address this question:
'Where do I need more momentum?' in relation to 'following' Jesus this month:

ADDITIONAL NOTES ON THIS PASSAGE:

LOOK: Where in this passage is God calling for my attention?

In the light of this, what might God be saying to me in at least one facet of my life? Circle one, or more, facet of your relationships: D N A

LISTEN: What is God up to? (in my life, or those around me).

LIVE: Where have I seen God at work?

LEARN: What am I learning from my experience over the past week?

This week make sure you address this question:
What practices shall we try this month?

ADDITIONAL NOTES ON THIS PASSAGE:

LOOK: Where in this passage is God calling for my attention?

In the light of this, what might God be saying to me in at least one facet of my life? Circle one, or more, facet of your relationships: D N A

LISTEN: What is God up to? (in my life, or those around me).

LIVE: Where have I seen God at work?

LEARN: What am I learning from my experience over the past week?

This week make sure you address this question:
Who are we praying for?

ADDITIONAL NOTES ON THIS PASSAGE:

AUTHENTICITY – week 4.   **MATTHEW 5:1-16.**

LOOK: Where in this passage is God calling for my attention?

In the light of this, what might God be saying to me in at least one facet of my life? Circle one, or more, facet of your relationships: D N A

LISTEN: What is God up to? (in my life, or those around me).

LIVE: Where have I seen God at work?

LEARN: What am I learning from my experience over the past week?

This week make sure you address this question:
How are we getting on with our practices?

ADDITIONAL NOTES ON THIS PASSAGE:

AUTHENTICITY – week 5.   **MATTHEW 5:1-16.**

LOOK: Where, primarily over this month, in this passage is God calling for my attention?

In the light of this, what might God be saying to me in at least one facet of my life? Circle one, or more, facet of your relationships: D N A

LISTEN: What, in summary this month, is God up to? (in my life, or those around me).

LIVE: Where, pre-dominantly this month, have I seen God at work?

LEARN: What, mainly, am I learning from my experience over the past month?
Which have you circled most this month (D,N, or A)?

This week make sure you address this question:
How can we encourage one another with our practices?

ADDITIONAL NOTES ON THIS PASSAGE:

HUMILITY.

.... from presumption to servanthood.

God grant me the serenity
To accept the things I cannot change;
Courage to change the things I can;
And wisdom to know the difference.

Living one day at a time;
Enjoying one moment at a time;
Accepting hardships as the pathway to peace;
Taking, as He did, this sinful world
As it is, not as I would have it;
Trusting that he will make all things right
If I surrender to His will;
That I may be reasonable happy in this life
And supremely happy with Him
Forever in the next.
Amen.

The Serenity Prayer by Reinhold Niebuhr.

'The Latin words humus, soil/earth, homo, and human being, have a common derivation, from which we also get our word "humble". This is the Genesis origin of who we are: dust – dust that the Lord God used to make us a human being. If we cultivate a lively sense of our origin and nurture a sense of continuity with it, who knows, we may also acquire humility'. – Eugene Peterson. [i]

'Do not think of yourself more highly than you ought, but rather think of yourself with sober judgment' Paul. [ii]

Humility is a virtue we shy away from. We fear it's like a bar of soap – if you try and grab hold of it, it'll slip away from our hands. Certainly, I know, to begin to think you are being humble is to raise the objections even from our own hearts. One of Winston Churchill's funniest quips concerned his political opponent, Clement Atlee. Churchill was interrupted by a friend who said, 'but surely, Mr Churchill, you admit that Mr Atlee is a humble man?' To which Churchill replies, 'He is a humble man, but then he has much to be humble about!' Not surprisingly, Churchill was often criticised for his own over confidence. Only when we see ourselves from a balanced perspective can we detect where growth in our humility is required. [iii]

Humility is a necessary facet of so many other virtues we are looking at developing more deeply in our lives over the course of a year. John Chrysostum said 'Humility is the garden of all virtues' and it remains a vivid metaphor, which highlights the crucial need for us all to allow the work of humility to become more deeply rooted in our hearts. For example, to be genuinely open towards other people requires humility. One of things we are struggling to learn, in the UK church context, is how our mission to others and communities is so often dependent upon their hospitality and welcome towards us, rather than the other way round. This necessitates humility, which may be why we are struggling so much.

If Chrysostum is right about the idea of humility being a garden, we might be wise to ask what needs to grow there to help it and what weeds need to be uprooted? Look at four areas:

i. Attitude – humility is an attitude, which needs to be cultivated. Wisdom has a key relationship to growing in humility. Pride, on the other hand, works against it (Proverbs 11:2; 15:33; 22:4. Colossians 2:18)). It is from the deep places of our own hearts' engagement, with the heart of God, that humility springs.

ii. Valuing others – humility is grown by valuing others more highly than yourself (Phil 2:3). Again it is pride, expressing itself in superiority, which works against it. I'm sure Paul never intended people to do this by devaluing themselves, but merely to work against what he describes as 'selfish ambition' and 'vain conceit'.

iii. Choice – it seems we have some choice in deciding whether to be humble, or not. (Psalm 45:4; Zephaniah 2:3; Colossians 3:12; James 3:13; 1 Peter 5:4-6).

iv. False humility – Paul warns us to guard against the impact of this upon us from other people (Colossians 2: 18,23). He does not see boldness opposing humility (2 Cor 10:1). It is vital, therefore, that we distinguish between true and counterfeit humility in our own hearts. Having the appearance of humility does not qualify for being the genuine article.

Only God sees us as we truly are. He reads our hearts more deeply, even than we might read a book, because he doesn't simply read what he finds, he knows the motivations behind each and every turn. This is good news, because I realise I am very adept at developing strategies to help me avoid facing the reality of who I am. I can fool myself sometimes, or at least try. So to nurture the ability to be honest with ourselves can save us a lot of heartache than leaving it to God to hold up the mirror. To do this we need to regard humility as our friend.

Lesslie Newbigin used to talk about 'bold humility', which, on first hearing, sounds a little odd. How do boldness and humility belong together in the same sentence? In many ways, however, bold humility is the only real antidote to false humility. Newbigin suggested we need to trust God enough to step out and speak boldly, but be humble enough to remember God works in ways that are more amazing than we could ever ask or imagine. This means, if we see our part in the mission of God as too significant, we shall lack the humility to allow God room to get in on and act in his play. If, on the other hand, we embrace false humility and simply go with our feelings of being worthless and assume we are incapable of doing anything significant in the name of Jesus, we shall miss engaging in the mission of God we are called to become co-workers in. Either way, it is humility, which can bring true perspective and keep us in the place where we can accept God's grace. CS Lewis brings a healthy warning: 'If anyone would like to acquire humility, I can, I think, tell him the first step. The first step is to realize that one is proud. And a biggish step too. At least, nothing whatever can be done before it. If you think you are not conceited, it means you are very conceited indeed.' [iv] It will sometimes feel as if we're walking on a tightrope with this one as it's easy to either overvalue what we're not, or undervalue what we are. All of us will lean one way, or the other. Which way for you?

One of the interesting things about Chaplains in the Royal Navy is their position in relation to the various ranks within the Navy. A Navy

Chaplain always assumes the rank of the person standing in front of them. So, when with an Admiral, there are to see themselves as an Admiral, but when with a lower ranking sea-man then they assume their rank. I wonder who I'd try and spend my time with the most!? It strikes me as a healthy way of countering the inner conflicts we so often have within our own hearts 'who is better?'; 'who is higher?'; 'who is better-off?'

Humility is mandated, but its expression is always culturally defined. Duane Elmer, in his delightful book, 'Cross-Cultural Servanthood' states: 'Humility is a mandated attitude for all believers everywhere; however, the way humility is expressed takes on a cultural face.' [v] The episode in which Jesus washes the feet of his disciples is one of the most graphic demonstrations of this and Jesus ends this by saying "Now I your Lord and Teacher, have washed your feet, you also should wash one another's feet. I have set you an example that you should do as I have done for you. Very truly I tell you, servants are not greater than their master, nor are messengers greater than the one who sent them. Now that you know these things, you will be blessed if you do them.' [vi]

One thing is very clear, from this passage alone, what is in the heart and mind of Jesus. He clearly expects his followers to act in the same way as he does. However, whilst foot washing was one very obvious way to demonstrate humility in his own cultural framework when walking this earth, it is not necessarily most appropriate for many cultures today. Particularly in the Western world, we fully understand this point, but maybe what we need to work on, as individuals, is finding ways to translate Jesus desire for us to express humility into our own cultures. More especially, what is required is for us to find ways by which we can express humility towards the other person in front of us.

There are clearly a whole variety of practices we might focus upon to encourage the spirit of humility in ourselves. By all means find your own, but if you're struggling I commend the practice of keeping short accounts as a good foundational starting place.

Keeping short accounts is about addressing any perceived growing gaps in our relationship with God and/or other people as soon as possible. Richard Foster talks about 'formation prayer' and he draws upon the Rule of St Benedict where Benedict discusses twelve steps into humility. [vii] Foster writes: 'Put in simple terms, humility means to live as close to the truth as possible: the truth about ourselves, the truth about others, the truth about the world in which we live.' [viii] Therefore, to establish, as part of our daily rhythm of prayer a time when we ask ourselves, before God, some simple questions will help enormously. Two questions might be:

- Where is there anxiety in my relationships? Is there anyone I have become aware of (including myself) where I am conscious something is pointing to the need for forgiveness, apology, openness, etc?

- Where might I need to act to put things right? It may well be all you need to do is in prayer between your own heart and God's. However, it may be that, sometimes you need to commit to God what you might need to say, or what you might need to initiate, with someone else.

Whilst Benedict was writing his Rule for monks living in community and in a very different age, there are some vital points he makes: Humility is primarily about our relationship with God. Again, we must recognise we cannot separate how we relate to God from our other relationships.
Humility can be grown. Benedict's steps are both spiritual and practical. Three concern the use of our tongue! Contentment in all things is another, which cuts through the heart of the values in our present age.

---

[i] Eugene Peterson. Christ Plays in Ten Thousand Places, Hodder and Stoughton, London, 2005, p76.

[ii] Romans 12:3.

[iii] cf: Romans 12:3.

[iv] CS Lewis. Mere Christianity, Macmillan, 1960, London, p99.

[v] Duane Elmer, Cross Cultural Servanthood, 2006, p33.

[vi] John 13: 14-17.

[vii] The Rule of St Benedict was produced by Benedict when Abbott of Monte Cassino.

[viii] Richard Foster, Prayer, Hodder and Stoughton London 1992. p63.

THE PASSAGE for this month: Mark 10: 32-45 is this month's passage. Listen to the same passage, at least each week when you meet together, asking where, or what, God is calling for your attention. Mark down, in the weekly table on the next page, which facet (at least one) of the following three areas of your relationships God might be speaking into:

D for discipleship – our relationship with God.
N for engagement – our relationship with others.
A for authenticity – our relationship with ourselves.

MY PRAYER FOCUS: The three people I am going to pray for, each week, this month, are:	
1	
2	
3	

MY PRACTISING: Additionally, read the material on "humility" and consider what you might 'practice' to develop what it means to engage more meaningfully with others in your own life:

1. What do I need to practice this month?
It is important you decide clearly what you're going to actually do. For example, don't vaguely write 'read a book', specify which book and how much you'll read per week.

2. When do I intend to practice?
Precisely 'when'. Will it be daily, weekly, etc. If you're dependent upon opportunities arising, when will you notice them?

3. How can I ensure I do practice?
A note in your diary, a regular time in a certain place, something else needing to go to make space? Most people can't simply add more time consuming items into already too busy schedules. Do I share in my DNA group what I'm doing and ask them to ask me in x weeks time, do I put a note in the diary to ask myself? etc.

HUMILITY - week 1.   MARK 10: 32-45.

LOOK: Where in this passage is God calling for my attention?

In the light of this, what might God be saying to me in at least one facet of my life? Circle one, or more, facet of your relationships: D N A

LISTEN: What is God up to? (in my life, or those around me).

LIVE: Where have I seen God at work?

LEARN: What am I learning from my experience over the past week?

This week make sure you address this question:
'Where do I need more momentum?' in relation to 'following' Jesus this month:

ADDITIONAL NOTES ON THIS PASSAGE:

LOOK:　　　Where in this passage is God calling for my attention?

In the light of this, what might God be saying to me in at least one facet of my life? Circle one, or more, facet of your relationships: D N A

LISTEN:　　What is God up to? (in my life, or those around me).

LIVE:　　　Where have I seen God at work?

LEARN:　　What am I learning from my experience over the past week?

This week make sure you address this question:
What practices shall we try this month?

ADDITIONAL NOTES ON THIS PASSAGE:

HUMILITY - week 3.   MARK 10: 32-45.

LOOK: Where in this passage is God calling for my attention?

In the light of this, what might God be saying to me in at least one facet of my life? Circle one, or more, facet of your relationships: D N A

LISTEN: What is God up to? (in my life, or those around me).

LIVE: Where have I seen God at work?

LEARN: What am I learning from my experience over the past week?

This week make sure you address this question:
Who are we praying for?

ADDITIONAL NOTES ON THIS PASSAGE:

LOOK: Where in this passage is God calling for my attention?

In the light of this, what might God be saying to me in at least one facet of my life? Circle one, or more, facet of your relationships: D N A

LISTEN: What is God up to? (in my life, or those around me).

LIVE: Where have I seen God at work?

LEARN: What am I learning from my experience over the past week?

This week make sure you address this question:
How are we getting on with our practices?

ADDITIONAL NOTES ON THIS PASSAGE:

HUMILITY - week 5.

LOOK: Where, primarily over this month, in this passage is God calling for my attention?

In the light of this, what might God be saying to me in at least one facet of my life? Circle one, or more, facet of your relationships: D N A

LISTEN: What, in summary this month, is God up to? (in my life, or those around me).

LIVE: Where, pre-dominantly this month, have I seen God at work?

LEARN: What, mainly, am I learning from my experience over the past month?
Which have you circled most this month (D,N, or A)?

This week make sure you address this question:
How can we encourage one another with our practices?

ADDITIONAL NOTES ON THIS PASSAGE:

LOOK: Where in this passage is God calling for my attention?

In the light of this, what might God be saying to me in at least one facet of my life? Circle one, or more, facet of your relationships: D N A

LISTEN: What is God up to? (in my life, or those around me).

LIVE: Where have I seen God at work?

LEARN: What am I learning from my experience over the past week?

This week make sure you address this question:
'Where do I need more momentum?' in relation to 'following' Jesus this month:

ADDITIONAL NOTES ON THIS PASSAGE:

LOOK: Where in this passage is God calling for my attention?

In the light of this, what might God be saying to me in at least one facet of my life? Circle one, or more, facet of your relationships: D N A

LISTEN: What is God up to? (in my life, or those around me).

LIVE: Where have I seen God at work?

LEARN: What am I learning from my experience over the past week?

This week make sure you address this question:
What practices shall we try this month?

ADDITIONAL NOTES ON THIS PASSAGE:

LOOK: Where in this passage is God calling for my attention?

In the light of this, what might God be saying to me in at least one facet of my life? Circle one, or more, facet of your relationships: D N A

LISTEN: What is God up to? (in my life, or those around me).

LIVE: Where have I seen God at work?

LEARN: What am I learning from my experience over the past week?

This week make sure you address this question:
Who are we praying for?

ADDITIONAL NOTES ON THIS PASSAGE:

AUTHENTICITY – week 4.   **MATTHEW 5:1-16.**

LOOK: Where in this passage is God calling for my attention?

In the light of this, what might God be saying to me in at least one facet of my life? Circle one, or more, facet of your relationships: D N A

LISTEN: What is God up to? (in my life, or those around me).

LIVE: Where have I seen God at work?

LEARN: What am I learning from my experience over the past week?

This week make sure you address this question:
How are we getting on with our practices?

ADDITIONAL NOTES ON THIS PASSAGE:

LOOK: Where, primarily over this month, in this passage is God calling for my attention?

In the light of this, what might God be saying to me in at least one facet of my life? Circle one, or more, facet of your relationships: D N A

LISTEN: What, in summary this month, is God up to? (in my life, or those around me).

LIVE: Where, pre-dominantly this month, have I seen God at work?

LEARN: What, mainly, am I learning from my experience over the past month?
Which have you circled most this month (D,N, or A)?

This week make sure you address this question:
How can we encourage one another with our practices?

ADDITIONAL NOTES ON THIS PASSAGE:

CULTIVATING

.... from programmer to environmentalist.

If we desperately need churches, which are organic, sustainable and reproducible, it sounds like we need some environmentalists to lead them!

The story of the re-introduction of the Red Kite into Britain is a thrilling story. Although Shakespeare once described London as 'a City of Red Kites and crows' they were on the brink of extinction in the UK. Their population declined largely due to them being treated as vermin destruction of their woodland habitats and poisoning. By the 1930's, apart from probably less than ten breeding pairs in Wales, they had become extinct in the whole of the UK. Today, however, there exists at least 2000 known breeding pairs. I cannot travel through Oxfordshire now without several sightings, although their re-introduction here only began about twenty years ago.

Question: How did things change?
Answer: A few dedicated people set about changing the environment in which Red Kites could successfully breed.

For growth to take place, every living system needs a sufficiently appropriate environment. This is why Christians need to be environmentalists and cultivators. Cultivation is a word commonly used among gardeners and farmers. It's about preparing the soil for whatever crops you desire to produce. It's concerned with improvement, development, nurturing and paying close attention to the environment. Interestingly, the definition of a cultivator is 'one who cultivates; implement or machine for breaking up ground and uprooting weeds'. [i]

Recently, Maggie and I joined the movement of allotment holders. Our excitement, on hearing our name had risen to the top of the list, soon waned when we saw how much work would be involved – just clearing the ground before we could think about planting a single seed! However, the thrill of seeing those first seeds burst through the ground will always remain. The biggest lesson I'm learning, slowly, is how important this whole business of cultivation really is. I go for the quick results – a quick dig over makes it all look great – lovely newly turned soil. However, unless Maggie comes along after me, and more effectively removes far more of the weeds than I ever see as necessary, we're back to square one, or worse. Cultivation is always hard work, (which is why I try and avoid it!) however, there are three key steps:

- **Preparing the ground.** This might mean digging, or ploughing. However, it also means removing weeds and other 'competitors' for the nutrients and space crops need.

- **Ensuring adequate essentials.** Choosing a good natural environment, which will provide sufficient amounts of sun, rain and soil nutrients is the key priority. However, careful observation will often necessitate the need to water, add nutrients to the soil, or protect from harsh weather.

- **Reading the seasons.** When to sow, when to harvest and when to prune. There are general patterns, which hold true every year for every crop. However, the most skilled of cultivators seem to just know, not simply 'how', but 'when'.

Read Ephesians 4 and ask yourself the question 'what is the primary role of a church leader as expressed here?' What is the skill someone needs to 'equip his people for works of service?'[ii] One word, which helpfully describes such a person is 'cultivator'. To cultivate an environment in which the kingdom of God can thrive is a key leadership role. I don't think one person alone can 'equip' everyone and Paul recognises this by stating his expectation of at least five ministries being required to accomplish this in any congregation. However, somebody needs to take responsibility for cultivating the appropriate environment in which others can grow.

Now think about the ministry of Jesus. Jesus had the habit of cultivating the environment for people, so they could find faith to enter the kingdom of God. How did he do this?

- **Preparing the ground.** Jesus was always preparing the hearts of people. Sometimes he challenged people directly to help them see where there good intentions were leading them astray. Sometimes he spoke in parables, which dropped an ever expanding clue, to the nature of God's kingdom, into people's hearts and minds. Sometimes he performed miraculous statements of God's kingdom for all to see.

- **Ensuring adequate essentials.** Sometimes Jesus provided a new perspective, which enables people, like the woman at the well, or the crowds at the feeding of the 5000, to see. Some people, like the rich young ruler, couldn't look at life through Jesus' lens. On other occasions Jesus offered the welcome, acceptance, or value people needed to take their next crucial step forward.

- **Reading the seasons.** Jesus spotted where people were in relation to the things of God and met them in that place. This is very different to sending an invitation to meet on church ground. Jesus reads our hearts and, consequently, approaches us according to where we are. However, this is never with a view to leaving us behind, that's just the starting point. When it seems the time is not 'now', Jesus provides the missing elements. He provides what people cannot find anywhere else: forgiveness. eternal hope and life, cleansing, the removal of shame and guilt, an alternative way to live our lives.

We're talking about developing the habit of creating space for other people. Jesus was a cultivator. He cultivated an environment in which everything we need for the mission of God to begin, or continue through us, is available. Whilst there are many aspects to being a cultivator, the practice I propose you focus upon this month, in following Jesus, is that of creating space for growth for others.

Think about those you regularly engage with, look back over those people you have regularly been praying for – what do they need to grow? It is widely recognised, today in the UK, people arrive at the place where they are confident in who Jesus is, as the result of a process. The 'crisis' point, we often refer to as our conversion, only typically arises after a sequence of other events, or phases of life and exploration. This seems obvious when you listen to the stories of new

Christians and wholly consistent to the work of the Holy Spirit as talked about by Jesus in various places. [iii]

What if God really is seeking to actively draw everybody to himself? Surely, looking at everyone, not simply as a person made in the image of God, but also as someone to whom God might be seeking to reveal the truth of his own self, makes a difference to how we both see and engage with them?

Many people have found the Engels scale a simple, but helpful, insight into some of the possible stages people go through en route to beginning to follow Jesus.

Engel's scale	GODS ROLE	CHURCH'S ROLE	HUMAN RESPONSE
-10	General revelation	Presence	Awareness of supernatural
-9			No effective knowledge of Christianity
-8	Conviction		Initial awareness of Christianity
-7			Interest in Christianity
-6		Proclamation	Awareness of basic facts of the gospel
-5			Grasp of implications of the gospel
-4			Positive attitude to the gospel
-3		Persuasion	Awareness of personal need
-2			Challenge and decision to act
-1	Regeneration		Repentance and faith
New start	New birth	New family	New hope

If Jesus is the centre – that is the one to whom all are being drawn, what might your role be to help people reach him?
We need to ensure we don't get in the way of anyone's route towards Jesus, as well as act as cultivators. Now, think about some of your

friends and ask yourself what actions, words and attitudes might cultivate an appropriate environment to make their journey towards Christ a little easier.

Preparing the ground, ensuring adequate essentials, or reading the seasons, for their next step towards Jesus, might include … (I suggest you fill in the blanks here!)

You'll soon see your response to any individual will be unique, but the desire to see their growth towards the people God intends them to become will be a common denominator. This is because the ways the gospel and kingdom are grown are essentially relational. Relationships need to be cultivated if they are to grow and be wholesome and authentic. If we can truly say we want the best for someone it quickly short-circuits the debates Christians get into (as a diversion, it seems to me, from actually getting to know anyone better) about whether our friendship with someone becomes tarnished in some way, if among the best we want for them means they become Christians.

Jesus cultivated life on different levels:

He lived out his life in such a way, which maintained a healthy balance nurturing both health and growth. Our own heart needs cultivation.
He removed the barriers from individuals lives, which they could not remove themselves. Others need to find the space to grow.
He provided an appropriate environment for health and growth for his disciples. Relationships need cultivation.
He cultivated an environment appropriate for the crowds, as well as his enemies, to see who he really was (if they chose to look) and hear his voice (if they chose to listen). Different groups have varying needs.
He cultivated a legacy, which has been attacked in every subsequent generation, but has never, nor ever shall, fail. Cultivation is not restricted to our ability.

My hope is your DNA group will become a mechanism to enable everyone involved to gradually feel they can pro-actively take responsibility for being cultivators.

Where are the Christian environmentalists? It's a tragedy, to me, the Church barely raises its voice in an arena which includes the biggest questions facing every human being on planet earth – its very future. Climate change, global warming, the future of the rain forests, re-cycling, sustainability, fair trade, the survival of species, ecological balance, etc. The list could go on, but these are big, big, issues which need to be of concern for us all, whether followers of Jesus, or not. One of the reasons the Church doesn't raise its voice in the environmental debate a great deal is because many Christians don't care enough – we still live with a wholly un-biblical perception we can divide life into compartments and, therefore, many people regard such concerns as 'unspiritual'. Surely, Christians have more to say, from God's perspective, than anyone? Couple this with the fact that environmental issues feature high on the list of the concerns with the younger generations, we not only have no excuses, but ignore such issues to the detriment of the missional stance I'd advocate should be normative for the Church.

---

[i] Definition taken from The Concise Oxford English Dictionary.
[ii] Ephesians 4:12.
[iii] The relationship between Jesus and the Holy Spirit appears as a dynamic, rather than static, one – eg: Luke 4:1,14,18. Our relationship with the Holy Spirit is intended to be equally dynamic – eg: John 3:5-8, John 6:63, John 14:15-31.

THE PASSAGE for this month: John 4: 1-23 is this month's passage. Listen to the same passage, at least each week when you meet together, asking where, or what, God is calling for your attention. Mark down, in the weekly table on the next page, which facet (at least one) of the following three areas of your relationships God might be speaking into:

D for discipleship – our relationship with God.
N for engagement – our relationship with others.
A for authenticity – our relationship with ourselves.

MY PRAYER FOCUS: The three people I am going to pray for, each week, this month, are:	
1	
2	
3	

MY PRACTISING: Additionally, read the material on "cultivating" and consider what you might 'practice' to develop what it means to engage more meaningfully with others in your own life:

1. What do I need to practice this month?
It is important you decide clearly what you're going to actually do. For example, don't vaguely write 'read a book', specify which book and how much you'll read per week.

2. When do I intend to practice?
Precisely 'when'. Will it be daily, weekly, etc. If you're dependent upon opportunities arising, when will you notice them?

3. How can I ensure I do practice?
A note in your diary, a regular time in a certain place, something else needing to go to make space? Most people can't simply add more time consuming items into already too busy schedules. Do I share in my DNA group what I'm doing and ask them to ask me in x weeks time, do I put a note in the diary to ask myself? etc.

LOOK: Where in this passage is God calling for my attention?

In the light of this, what might God be saying to me in at least one facet of my life? Circle one, or more, facet of your relationships: D N A

LISTEN: What is God up to? (in my life, or those around me).

LIVE: Where have I seen God at work?

LEARN: What am I learning from my experience over the past week?

This week make sure you address this question:
'Where do I need more momentum?' in relation to 'following' Jesus this month:

ADDITIONAL NOTES ON THIS PASSAGE:

LOOK:　　　Where in this passage is God calling for my attention?

In the light of this, what might God be saying to me in at least one facet of my life? Circle one, or more, facet of your relationships: D N A

LISTEN:　　What is God up to? (in my life, or those around me).

LIVE:　　　Where have I seen God at work?

LEARN:　　What am I learning from my experience over the past week?

This week make sure you address this question:
What practices shall we try this month?

ADDITIONAL NOTES ON THIS PASSAGE:

LOOK: Where in this passage is God calling for my attention?

In the light of this, what might God be saying to me in at least one facet of my life? Circle one, or more, facet of your relationships: D N A

LISTEN: What is God up to? (in my life, or those around me).

LIVE: Where have I seen God at work?

LEARN: What am I learning from my experience over the past week?

This week make sure you address this question:
Who are we praying for?

ADDITIONAL NOTES ON THIS PASSAGE:

CULTIVATING - week 4.   JOHN 4: 1-23.

LOOK: Where in this passage is God calling for my attention?

In the light of this, what might God be saying to me in at least one facet of my life? Circle one, or more, facet of your relationships: D N A

LISTEN: What is God up to? (in my life, or those around me).

LIVE: Where have I seen God at work?

LEARN: What am I learning from my experience over the past week?

This week make sure you address this question:
How are we getting on with our practices?

ADDITIONAL NOTES ON THIS PASSAGE:

CULTIVATING – week 5.

LOOK: Where, primarily over this month, in this passage is God calling for my attention?

In the light of this, what might God be saying to me in at least one facet of my life? Circle one, or more, facet of your relationships: D N A

LISTEN: What, in summary this month, is God up to? (in my life, or those around me).

LIVE: Where, pre-dominantly this month, have I seen God at work?

LEARN: What, mainly, am I learning from my experience over the past month?
Which have you circled most this month (D,N, or A)?

This week make sure you address this question:
How can we encourage one another with our practices?

ADDITIONAL NOTES ON THIS PASSAGE:

AUTHENTICITY - week 1.   MATTHEW 5:1-16.

LOOK: Where in this passage is God calling for my attention?

In the light of this, what might God be saying to me in at least one facet of my life? Circle one, or more, facet of your relationships: D N A

LISTEN: What is God up to? (in my life, or those around me).

LIVE: Where have I seen God at work?

LEARN: What am I learning from my experience over the past week?

This week make sure you address this question:
'Where do I need more momentum?' in relation to 'following' Jesus this month:

ADDITIONAL NOTES ON THIS PASSAGE:

AUTHENTICITY - week 2.   **MATTHEW 5:1-16.**

LOOK: Where in this passage is God calling for my attention?

In the light of this, what might God be saying to me in at least one facet of my life? Circle one, or more, facet of your relationships: D N A

LISTEN: What is God up to? (in my life, or those around me).

LIVE: Where have I seen God at work?

LEARN: What am I learning from my experience over the past week?

This week make sure you address this question:
What practices shall we try this month?

ADDITIONAL NOTES ON THIS PASSAGE:

LOOK: Where in this passage is God calling for my attention?

In the light of this, what might God be saying to me in at least one facet of my life? Circle one, or more, facet of your relationships: D N A

LISTEN: What is God up to? (in my life, or those around me).

LIVE: Where have I seen God at work?

LEARN: What am I learning from my experience over the past week?

This week make sure you address this question:
Who are we praying for?

ADDITIONAL NOTES ON THIS PASSAGE:

LOOK: Where in this passage is God calling for my attention?

In the light of this, what might God be saying to me in at least one facet of my life? Circle one, or more, facet of your relationships: D N A

LISTEN: What is God up to? (in my life, or those around me).

LIVE: Where have I seen God at work?

LEARN: What am I learning from my experience over the past week?

This week make sure you address this question:
How are we getting on with our practices?

ADDITIONAL NOTES ON THIS PASSAGE:

AUTHENTICITY – week 5.   MATTHEW 5:1-16.

LOOK: Where, primarily over this month, in this passage is God calling for my attention?

In the light of this, what might God be saying to me in at least one facet of my life? Circle one, or more, facet of your relationships: D N A

LISTEN: What, in summary this month, is God up to? (in my life, or those around me).

LIVE: Where, pre-dominantly this month, have I seen God at work?

LEARN: What, mainly, am I learning from my experience over the past month?
Which have you circled most this month (D,N, or A)?

This week make sure you address this question:
How can we encourage one another with our practices?

ADDITIONAL NOTES ON THIS PASSAGE:

ENDURANCE

.... from comfort to adventure.

Old men ought to be explorers
Here or there does not matter:
We must be still and still moving. TS Eliot.

Never stop exploring - add your name here!

Looking back over the last ten years of your life, what do you wish
you had not given up?
Do you wish you'd pursued your education beyond the initial poor
marks, or stayed on longer before leaving?
Do you look back on childhood opportunities to learn a musical
instrument, or sport you couldn't be bothered with?
Do you wish you'd persevered in a relationship, beyond the pain
barrier when things got a bit rocky?
Do you regret you've never grown as much into what you'd always
imagined a normal Christian life would become?

'If at first you don't succeed .... then maybe failure is your thing.'
I realise the ending to the old adage is 'then try, try, try again'. Most
people don't .... with anything! Most people try something once, don't
like it, or don't succeed, from their perspective, and give up. Observe
this wherever you look – education, sport, food, music, etc. Following
Jesus, however, provides us with a real opportunity to become more
than we are. You are not most people.

Like me, you may wish to claim, it was a lack of ability, which kept me
from mastering the guitar. However, a lack of endurance is at the root
of many of our past regrets. Check out the parable of the sower and
see how important endurance is in our relationship with God. [i]
Express your gratitude, also, to Jesus, who 'for the joy that was set
before him endured the cross, scorning its shame'. [ii] It's as we look at
Jesus' life, we find the clues to building endurance in our own lives.

Endurance in the present is grown by focusing on the horizon ahead.
Our 'instant society' context often requires a conscious reminder
nothing worthwhile is gained instantly. Even the grace of God, whilst

available in an instant, takes a lifetime of un-packing and is never a by-pass around pain, or suffering.

Don't be fooled into thinking endurance is anybody else's challenge, but your own. Sebastian Coe, winner of two Olympic gold medals for Great Britain, stated 'throughout my athletics career, the overall aim was always to be a better athlete than I was at that moment – whether next week, next month, or next year. The improvement was the goal. The medal was simply the ultimate reward for achieving that goal.' [iii]

Work – how many times have you worded your resignation letter in your head? It's usually when the pressure is mounting from deadlines, demands, or dreariness. If you don't walk out at that point you stand to develop endurance.

Relationships - not necessarily relationships, which have come to an end. Where have you settled - for an easy time, convenience, or fear – in your relationships? We often miss the growth points because one steps back from facing the pain barrier. Things seldom 'just get better' and, often get worse, before improvement begins.

Character – look around at your friends. Those you cherish the most are likely to be those who have qualities of endurance in their relationship … with us! This is suggesting we try and help others produce endurance by being a pain in their neck! It is suggesting we watch, learn and apply what we see there. Others will, more likely, include you in their list if you become someone who can endure.

Spirituality – how many promises has God heard from you about praying more consistently, reading your Bible more regularly and demonstrating acts of kindness more than haphazardly? The likelihood is it's a lack of endurance, which has thwarted us and not a deeply unwilling, or unspiritual, nature.

Endurance is never grown without pain, or hardship. There are no short-cuts. It doesn't happen by reading about it, or listening to someone else. If you simply carry on when you don't want to quit, it's not endurance you're producing. Endurance only grows when you *do want to quit*. We all have a pain barrier – when everything within you suggests 'pack it in and stop trying to go further forward' – where's yours?

Becoming a Christian will be a disappointment! It sounds wrong, but in following Jesus we soon become disappointed in him and with ourselves. Of course, Jesus is the only perfect example of a human being to have walked this earth, but our expectations of who he is and what he'll do (usually for us) are prone to lead us to disappointment. If, however, this leads us to discover more of who Jesus *really* is then it will be a significant place of discovery and growth. The real Jesus never disappoints, but the counterfeit copies we construct, to serve our needs, always will. Facing our disappointments can provide us with a springboard to the next level we wont easily find elsewhere. Unfortunately, the quick-fix cultural expectations have been imported into the Church, where they don't belong.

Whether it's Julie Andrews, (aka Mary Poppins) who said 'perseverance is failing nineteen times and succeeding the twentieth', or Winston Churchill, who said 'never, never, never, never give up …. I am sure of this, that you have only to endure to conquer'. History is littered with great people whose 'greatness' only happened because they persevered where most give up.

Abraham Lincoln is one of my favourite examples: In 1816, he had to work to support his family after they were forced out of their home. In 1816, his mother died. In 1831, he failed in business. In 1832, he was defeated for legislature, he lost his job and couldn't get into law school. In 1833, he was declared bankrupt and spent the next 17 years of his life paying off the money he borrowed from friends to start his business. In 1834, he was defeated for legislature again. In 1835, his fiancée died, which broke his heart. In 1836, he had a nervous breakdown and spent the next six months in bed. In 1836, he was defeated in becoming the speaker of the state legislature. In 1840, he was defeated in becoming elector. In 1843, 1846 and 1848 he was defeated for Congress. In 1849 he was rejected for the job of Land Officer in his home state. In 1854, he was defeated for Senate. In 1856, he was defeated for Vice-President, getting less than 100 votes. In 1858, he was defeated for Senate for the third time. In 1860, he elected President of the United States and 'destined' to become one of the most significant ever. Dare you answer when you would have given up?

'Endurance' was the name given by Sir Ernest Shackleton to the ship, which he used for his most notorious adventure, but he embodied endurance in a way few others ever get near. Shackleton has been described as 'the greatest leader that ever came on God's earth, bar none' for saving the lives of the twenty-seven men stranded with him on an Antarctic ice floe for almost two years. [iv] Ironically, and this is why Shackleton can be such an inspirational mentor, he failed to reach nearly every goal he ever set!

- He failed as part of a three man team to reach the South Pole in 1902.
- He failed leading his own team six years later a heart-breaking 97 miles short of the Pole, but only after realising it would mean certain starvation for his team to carry on.
- He failed in his 1914-1916 Endurance expedition. He lost his ship before even touching Antarctica.

His story is no glorification of failure, there are plenty of 'successes', he 'failed only at the improbable; he succeeded at the unimaginable' [v]

Only recently has Shackleton become regarded as an example of what it takes to be a great leader and three reasons why I believe his example has so much to teach us are:

i.   In a rapidly changing world he was always willing to venture in new directions to seize new opportunities and learn new skills.
ii. He learnt most about success through failure.
iii. He invested in other people.

'Endurance' was his family motto 'By endurance we conquer', but what makes his story remarkable is the way he embodied it. So often, perseverance is what sets us apart. What we need to grasp is no one respected for their success has ever found it without failure and, therefore, endurance. So, think of the people whose achievements you admire. Now think again - endurance usually plays a significant part.

Endurance tends to develop within us as a result of challenge, the need for growth and development, or in response to something negative. Endurance is a character issue, so it's highly unlikely someone will persevere in only one aspect of their life. However, giving up and become endemic - if we give up one thing easily it's often not the only thing. The good news is, whilst not born with perseverance in-built, it's something God will help grow within us, but how does this develop in ordinary people like us?

i. Choose wise priorities. Jesus didn't attempt to persevere in everything and with everyone. We need God's wisdom to realise where our best efforts need to go.

ii. Disappointment can be the death of perseverance – but only of we let it. If you identify an aspect of your life where you recognise you've stopped trying to persevere, look for the root of disappointment. Disappointed with God? Ourselves? One another?

iii. Overcoming fear – fear inhibits and stagnates growth within. Fear has many guises and is not dealt with by pretending it's not there. Identified, owned it can be dealt with. Fear of failing again as a result of our past experiences is a common enemy of developing perseverance and talking it out is often a good place to start.

iv. Focusing ahead develops present endurance – if we're too weighed down with where we've got to, we don't persevere, or endure. Seeing where you're headed and knowing what the next step of faith might look like you need to take are good antidotes. Look for these four factors in the following passage:

'Therefore, since we are surrounded by such a great cloud of witnesses, let us throw off everything that hinders and the sin that so easily entangles. And let us run with perseverance the race marked out for us, fixing our eyes upon Jesus, the pioneer and perfecter of faith. For the joy that was set before him he endured the cross, scorning its shame, and sat down at the right hand of the throne of God. Consider him who endured such opposition from sinners, so that you will not grow weary and lose heart.'

One of the most effective practices for developing perseverance is what we've been doing by meeting together in our DNA group to gather around the person of Jesus. – fixing our eyes upon Jesus and considering him. You may find it worthwhile to carve out some time, even now, and reflect on your experience of focusing upon Jesus and its impact upon this aspect of your life.

Some ways the DNA group you belong to can provide a real impetus to developing endurance:

i. Simply knowing somebody knows is a massive encouragement.
ii. Anticipating somebody will ask 'how's it going' is a great incentive.
iii. Confessing our sin to another person can lessen its hold upon us.
iv. Receiving prayer for God's help bridges the gap between the eternal dimension and what we often think of as the ordinary, here and now.

However, the practice I'm suggesting you give a go this month, to root the idea of fixing your eyes on Jesus, is journaling. I'm sure some people will be disappointed it's not something more adventurous such as running a marathon, or swimming the channel, but just think about it for a moment. How many people have ever tried to keep a diary, but failed? Pretty much everyone I ever speak to. Think, however, how you ever notice growth? Children get fed up with adults who they see infrequently telling them 'wow how you've grown'! However, all their doing is noticing what we miss when we're with them all the time – the kind of difference two photos taken months, or years, apart reveals.

Journaling is simply the means. In one sense it's a spiritual diary. However, unlike Bridget Jones, I suggest you keep it to yourself! Over time journaling is one way, which can help us detect what God has been saying over a longer period of time. In one sense it's merely building on the very simple building blocks you're accumulating by filling in some brief responses to the passages and practices as a result of being in a DNA group. Look back over a few months and you may begin to detect a pattern. This could be an indication of God repeating a similar message, or highlighting a particular aspect of life. I remember some one talking to me about how they were struggling. It was not the first conversation and it was a result of what was, by now obvious to me, a familiar pattern – overwork leading to stress leading to physical symptoms leading to time off work leading more stress about not doing enough work. The simple question 'what do you think God might be saying to you about this cycle?' was an obvious one to ask, but clearly not one being asked by the person in front of me. Journaling, on one level, helps us ask that question by enabling an overview of a longer period of our life than we habitually have.

I'm not a natural, don't write a daily journal and don't find it easy. I do, however, keep a notebook in which I put a whole variety of things as they strike me: thoughts, ideas, quotes, stories, bible references, comments on my bible study, doodles, questions I need to attend to, intentions, hopes, dreams. Looking back I can see some my clearest steps forward have been helped by the seed being first expressed in my 'journal'. To be honest, I didn't get into this with much enthusiasm. Then one Christmas my daughter, Emily, bought me one of those little books of blank pages. She knew I loved the look of them and had seen me scribbling notes here, there and everywhere and so gave me one with the inscription… 'sorry if this is a little random, but thought it might be useful for your little scribbles/doodles …. Well, use it as you wish, enjoy!' To be honest, it's one of the best presents I've ever had. I can look through it now and see the threads God has woven into my life as a result. I keep my notebook with my bible, so when I'm reading and praying alone, I can make use of it, although I use it elsewhere as well. It's provided me with one thing in particular: a greater view of God's perspective on my life as a result of an intentional expression of what God is doing inside of me.

Simply by writing something down:

- I own what's going on inside.
- I'm more likely to not forget, even if it's months later.
- I can look at it more clearly.
- I'm more likely to do something about it.
- I make myself accountable to my own hopes and dreams.

- I'm less likely to give up – keep it to myself and I can fool myself more easily than if it's in my journal. My journal knows! Daft it may sound, but it's simply a device, which no one else will ever see, but may help us face the reality of our own heart before God more easily.
- I'm less likely to avoid, or bury the questions I've posed, or been asked by God.

So, buy a notebook, find your own way, don't set yourself an unrealistic target, don't feel obliged to write something every day, do make it work for you, write whatever and wherever God leads your imagination and thinking and, as Emily said, 'enjoy'!

Pilgrim:
when your ship,
long moored in harbour,
gives you the illusion
of being a house;
when your ship
begins to put down roots
in the stagnant water by the quay:
put out to sea!
Save your boat's journeying soul,
and your own pilgrim soul,
cost what it may. [vi]

---

[i] Matthew 13:1-24.
[ii] Hebrews 12:2.
[iii] TV interview with Sebastian Coe.
[iv] Margot Morrell and Stephanie Capparell, *Shackleton's Way*, Nicholas Brealey Publishing, 2001, p1.
[v] Ibid., p1.
[vi] Dom Helder Camara From A Thousand Reasons for Living (London: Darton, Longman and Todd, 1981) p 40.

THE PASSAGE for this month: John 14 is this month's passage. Listen to the same passage, at least each week when you meet together, asking where, or what, God is calling for your attention. Mark down, in the weekly table on the next page, which facet (at least one) of the following three areas of your relationships God might be speaking into:

D for discipleship – our relationship with God.
N for engagement – our relationship with others.
A for authenticity – our relationship with ourselves.

MY PRAYER FOCUS: The three people I am going to pray for, each week, this month, are:	
1	
2	
3	

MY PRACTISING: Additionally, read the material on "endurance" and consider what you might 'practice' to develop what it means to engage more meaningfully with others in your own life:

1. What do I need to practice this month?
It is important you decide clearly what you're going to actually do. For example, don't vaguely write 'read a book', specify which book and how much you'll read per week.

2. When do I intend to practice?
Precisely 'when'. Will it be daily, weekly, etc. If you're dependent upon opportunities arising, when will you notice them?

3. How can I ensure I do practice?
A note in your diary, a regular time in a certain place, something else needing to go to make space? Most people can't simply add more time consuming items into already too busy schedules. Do I share in my DNA group what I'm doing and ask them to ask me in x weeks time, do I put a note in the diary to ask myself? etc.

LOOK: Where in this passage is God calling for my attention?

In the light of this, what might God be saying to me in at least one facet of my life? Circle one, or more, facet of your relationships: D N A

LISTEN: What is God up to? (in my life, or those around me).

LIVE: Where have I seen God at work?

LEARN: What am I learning from my experience over the past week?

This week make sure you address this question:
'Where do I need more momentum?' in relation to 'following' Jesus this month:

ADDITIONAL NOTES ON THIS PASSAGE:

LOOK: Where in this passage is God calling for my attention?

In the light of this, what might God be saying to me in at least one facet of my life? Circle one, or more, facet of your relationships: D N A

LISTEN: What is God up to? (in my life, or those around me).

LIVE: Where have I seen God at work?

LEARN: What am I learning from my experience over the past week?

This week make sure you address this question:
What practices shall we try this month?

ADDITIONAL NOTES ON THIS PASSAGE:

LOOK: Where in this passage is God calling for my attention?

In the light of this, what might God be saying to me in at least one facet of my life? Circle one, or more, facet of your relationships: D N A

LISTEN: What is God up to? (in my life, or those around me).

LIVE: Where have I seen God at work?

LEARN: What am I learning from my experience over the past week?

This week make sure you address this question:
Who are we praying for?

ADDITIONAL NOTES ON THIS PASSAGE:

LOOK: Where in this passage is God calling for my attention?

In the light of this, what might God be saying to me in at least one facet of my life? Circle one, or more, facet of your relationships: D N A

LISTEN: What is God up to? (in my life, or those around me).

LIVE: Where have I seen God at work?

LEARN: What am I learning from my experience over the past week?

This week make sure you address this question:
How are we getting on with our practices?

ADDITIONAL NOTES ON THIS PASSAGE:

LOOK: Where, primarily over this month, in this passage is God calling for my attention?

In the light of this, what might God be saying to me in at least one facet of my life? Circle one, or more, facet of your relationships: D N A

LISTEN: What, in summary this month, is God up to? (in my life, or those around me).

LIVE: Where, pre-dominantly this month, have I seen God at work?

LEARN: What, mainly, am I learning from my experience over the past month?
Which have you circled most this month (D,N, or A)?

This week make sure you address this question:
How can we encourage one another with our practices?

ADDITIONAL NOTES ON THIS PASSAGE:

AUTHENTICITY - week 1.   **MATTHEW 5:1-16.**

LOOK: Where in this passage is God calling for my attention?

In the light of this, what might God be saying to me in at least one facet of my life? Circle one, or more, facet of your relationships: D N A

LISTEN: What is God up to? (in my life, or those around me).

LIVE: Where have I seen God at work?

LEARN: What am I learning from my experience over the past week?

This week make sure you address this question:
'Where do I need more momentum?' in relation to 'following' Jesus this month:

ADDITIONAL NOTES ON THIS PASSAGE:

AUTHENTICITY - week 2.   **MATTHEW 5:1-16.**

LOOK: Where in this passage is God calling for my attention?

In the light of this, what might God be saying to me in at least one facet of my life? Circle one, or more, facet of your relationships: D N A

LISTEN: What is God up to? (in my life, or those around me).

LIVE: Where have I seen God at work?

LEARN: What am I learning from my experience over the past week?

This week make sure you address this question:
What practices shall we try this month?

ADDITIONAL NOTES ON THIS PASSAGE:

LOOK: Where in this passage is God calling for my attention?

In the light of this, what might God be saying to me in at least one facet of my life? Circle one, or more, facet of your relationships: D N A

LISTEN: What is God up to? (in my life, or those around me).

LIVE: Where have I seen God at work?

LEARN: What am I learning from my experience over the past week?

This week make sure you address this question:
Who are we praying for?

ADDITIONAL NOTES ON THIS PASSAGE:

AUTHENTICITY - week 4.   MATTHEW 5:1-16.

LOOK: Where in this passage is God calling for my attention?

In the light of this, what might God be saying to me in at least one facet of my life? Circle one, or more, facet of your relationships: D N A

LISTEN: What is God up to? (in my life, or those around me).

LIVE: Where have I seen God at work?

LEARN: What am I learning from my experience over the past week?

This week make sure you address this question:
How are we getting on with our practices?

ADDITIONAL NOTES ON THIS PASSAGE:

LOOK: Where, primarily over this month, in this passage is God calling for my attention?

In the light of this, what might God be saying to me in at least one facet of my life? Circle one, or more, facet of your relationships: D N A

LISTEN: What, in summary this month, is God up to? (in my life, or those around me).

LIVE: Where, pre-dominantly this month, have I seen God at work?

LEARN: What, mainly, am I learning from my experience over the past month?
Which have you circled most this month (D,N, or A)?

This week make sure you address this question:
How can we encourage one another with our practices?

ADDITIONAL NOTES ON THIS PASSAGE:

ATTENTIVENESS

.... from rushing to abiding.

'Hurry is not of the devil, it is the devil'. [i]

'Jesus is the centre of all, the object of all, whoever does not know him, knows nothing aright, either of the world, or of himself.' – Blaise Pascal.

In month one, we attempted to practise our listening skills. I wonder how you done? In 2005, The Bible Society sponsored the Bible reading questions used by the English Church Census, which is the largest and most thorough-going access to statistics on the UK Church we have. Altogether 27% of churchgoers in England, in 2005, claimed to read the Bible personally at least once a week, outside of church services, (in the United States it's 45%). The question this provoked in my mind was: to what extent is the current crisis in the British Church a result of not paying attention to the voice of Jesus? Attentiveness will be our focus this month.

Primarily, because the strand of DNA we're focusing upon again is our own need for authenticity, we shall consider the challenge of being attentive to our own heart before God. However, attentiveness is a posture we need, also, in relation to both the voice of God and the people around us. Each is intimately linked to the extent we practise attentiveness to our own heart. Jesus says: 'out of the overflow of the heart the mouth speaks'. [ii]

Pay attention!
How many times have we heard those words, I wonder? Maybe, because we heard them at school too frequently, in a stern voice from our teachers, we hear them negatively. However, words of warning are not, of necessity, negative:
The parent saying: 'listen that fire is dangerous' to their child.
The warning light on the car dashboard saying: 'fill up, before you run dry'.
Jesus saying 'do not', 'ask', 'enter', watch out', 'not everyone', 'practice', etc. [iii]

So what is it we need to pay attention to in our heart right now? It will be different for each of us on any one day and clearly vary, for ourselves, from day to day. I have a deep concern, however, too few people dare to ask the question for fear of what they might find, or knowing this not wishing to face their reality. To ask the question is the biggest, but first step we take towards attentiveness.

Mind the gap.

We hear it on the Underground and it's been the source of much amusement. Michael Palin once wrote 'the most famous phrase associated with the London Underground, must surely have the creators of the system spinning in their graves. It's an acknowledgement that the thing doesn't quite work. That however fast and frequent the service, however comprehensive the network, the trains don't always fit the platforms.' [iv]

When it comes to the gap between our heart and the heart of God, this gap grows if not attended to. Our month on authenticity was a focus on bringing the parts, which make up who we are, together as a more consistent whole. Openness is about helping people see underneath our superficial surface. Humility is concerned with developing a realistic and honest appraisal of who we are. Attentiveness is a habit, which needs to be applied to each of these facets, but being attentive to our heart, needs to be focused upon reducing the gap between the inside and the outside.

Attentiveness must become intentional.

I have come to the conclusion very little happens without intentionality. I've often heard it said 'you don't get what you expect, you only get what you inspect'. I confess I believed the theory a long time before I began to apply it in my own life. It's also easier to apply it to everyone else! So, I reluctantly admit, there needs to be some personal intentionality for it to happen. Attentiveness brings what's often there already into focus and, if that is to happen, it requires discipline. We are the only ones who'll make it happen in our lives: fact.

Have you noticed how so many voices are competing for our attention, so much information attempting to fill the capacity of our minds, so many demands trying to fill our time, so many opportunities awaiting someone to give them a go …. there's too much for any one life. The challenge for many within the western world today is certainly not trying to find something to do, learn, or experience, but sifting out what is worth giving our lives to.

What would Jesus do?

This is a great question, to ask ourselves on a regular basis as an antidote to the myriad of daily distractions blurring our focus upon Jesus too much. Sadly, it's one which has been relegated to the wristbands of young people - as if you can grow out of it! I agree wholeheartedly with Michael Frost and Alan Hirsch when they say we need to re-calibrate our movement around its founder: Jesus. The very first question they pose in their book ReJesus is 'what on-going role does Jesus the Messiah play in shaping the ethos and self-understanding of the movement that originated in him? [v] The words of Jesus are the most challenging we'll ever hear, but there's always the real danger we study the life out of the Bible. DNA groups are one way of putting more emphasis on allowing the voice of God getting to our ears before we explain it away and lose its edge. Now is a good time, when you've hopefully been regularly exploring your Christian DNA for a year, to reflect on where you have grown as a disciple. Keep, keeping on is the way ahead. It was Vincent Van Gogh, the Dutch nineteenth century artist, who said 'great things are not done by impulse, but by a series of small things brought together.' I'd be surprised if you've been challenged to do anything, as a result of being part of your group, you were not already aware of. It's now however our awareness of information, which changes us, but its' embodiment and practical expression in living it out.

Practicing attentiveness.

How on earth do we do this when the object is our own heart? As with every other month, I shall propose you concentrate upon one practice, but, as ever, acknowledge there is not one way to develop this habit. Leighton Ford's book, 'The Attentive Life' is a recommended read and in every chapter he has a section on 'practicing attentiveness', so you could fine nine there just for starters! However, I'm proposing the practice of holding silence as your starting point.

Holding silence.

Holding silence is not the same as having nothing to say. Admittedly, holding silence will be a harder practice to establish for those of us, myself included, who often only discover what we're thinking as a result of hearing our own voice. Even so, deliberately holding silence is not automatically easier for those who are naturally shy in a crowd, or frequently feel they have nothing to say in a group. Holding silence is challenging for introverts and extroverts alike simply because of the challenge of how we use the silence. It is in the silence, created by holding our own tongue, (or perhaps even our silent tongue – we will all know how easy it is to be pretending to listen to someone else, whilst we are actually inwardly listening to our own agenda). In this silence, we can better pay attention to the relationship between our heart and the heart of God.

I am a birdwatcher, but I don't frequently go somewhere special, sit in a hide for hours on end and watch patiently. My bird-watching is done wherever and whenever. What constantly amazes me is how many people, after I suddenly interject a conversation with 'look at that buzzard', or did you see that kingfisher?' who just simply do not 'see' any birds at all. I can't understand it, they're around us all the time. I have concluded they are only seen by those with eyes to see. For me, it's instinctive, I don't feel I need to look, I just see them. Something similar goes on when we look for where God is at work in our own lives. Many Christians spend many years oblivious to what God is up to, even through them. So many people are surprised when someone comments they can see God at work, as a result of their words, or actions. Jesus only did what he saw the Father doing also. [vi]For that to happen demanded Jesus paid attention to what he saw around him. With practice we will spot God at work more readily, but holding silence ourselves may be the way we find the space to see.

So when you next ask someone a question, hold silence. Give them space to answer, even if they don't within 10 seconds! In your DNA group, concentrate a little more on holding back and allowing the others to find God. The Psalmist is revealing something precious when he passes on the advice 'be still and know that I am God'. [vii] When God next highlights something you need to pay attention to in your own life, hold it. Hang on to what you sense you are being told, before you jump in with your excuses. Even if you acknowledge your need to be forgiven, spend some time looking for what might have been behind your wrong-doing in the first place. Action, or words, after holding silence is invariably more focused as a result. However, unless what we sense, or hear from God is not written down, or in some other way reinforced, we frequently lose its intended impact. The episode in Moby Dick is a fascinating insight when it says, speaking of the harpoonist,

As it's the twelfth month, I might dare to suggest an extra simple practice this month, which is simply thanksgiving. To climb into bed each night, thankful to God for something specific, brings a perspective to any day, which roots us in gratitude to God. Ray Brown, who was the Principal of Spurgeon's College when I attended, taught this. I can't claim to have practiced every night, but certainly many. On a good day it reminds me I am a grateful recipient of the grace of God. On a bad day it reminds me the grace of God has been made real to me and is deeper than any hole I may have found myself in. Whatever the day, to pay attention to God's faithfulness towards us brings a bigger perspective than the one we create, left to our own devices. As you look back over this last year, I hope you can see you are on an exciting adventure of discovery with God. We'll all have a long way to go, but I'm glad you're on the move.

Onwards and upwards. [viii]

---

[i] C G Jung, I think, source unknown

[ii] Luke 6:45.

[iii] All of these are found in Matthew chapter 7, but there are many other examples to be found!

[iv] Mind the Gap, Harper Collins, London, 2001, Simon James, Foreword by Michael Palin.

[v] ReJesus. A wild Messiah for a Missional Church. Michael Frost and Alan Hirsch. Hendrickson Publishers 2009 p5. These two delightful Australians have written some great stuff for those who are willing to spend some time trying to understand, not only about how we've got into such a mess in the western church, but also how we might begin to re-configure the church around Jesus.

[vi] John

[vii] Psalm 46:10.

[viii]

THE PASSAGE for this month: Matthew 7 is this month's passage. Listen to the same passage, at least each week when you meet together, asking where, or what, God is calling for your attention. Mark down, in the weekly table on the next page, which facet (at least one) of the following three areas of your relationships God might be speaking into:

D for discipleship – our relationship with God.
N for engagement – our relationship with others.
A for authenticity – our relationship with ourselves.

MY PRAYER FOCUS: The three people I am going to pray for, each week, this month, are:	
1	
2	
3	

MY PRACTISING: Additionally, read the material on "attentiveness" and consider what you might 'practice' to develop what it means to engage more meaningfully with others in your own life:

1. What do I need to practice this month?
It is important you decide clearly what you're going to actually do. For example, don't vaguely write 'read a book', specify which book and how much you'll read per week.

2. When do I intend to practice?
Precisely 'when'. Will it be daily, weekly, etc. If you're dependent upon opportunities arising, when will you notice them?

3. How can I ensure I do practice?
A note in your diary, a regular time in a certain place, something else needing to go to make space? Most people can't simply add more time consuming items into already too busy schedules. Do I share in my DNA group what I'm doing and ask them to ask me in x weeks time, do I put a note in the diary to ask myself? etc.

ATTENTIVENESS – week 1.   MATTHEW 7.

LOOK: Where in this passage is God calling for my attention?

In the light of this, what might God be saying to me in at least one facet of my life? Circle one, or more, facet of your relationships: D N A

LISTEN: What is God up to? (in my life, or those around me).

LIVE: Where have I seen God at work?

LEARN: What am I learning from my experience over the past week?

This week make sure you address this question:
'Where do I need more momentum?' in relation to 'following' Jesus this month:

ADDITIONAL NOTES ON THIS PASSAGE:

LOOK: Where in this passage is God calling for my attention?

In the light of this, what might God be saying to me in at least one facet of my life? Circle one, or more, facet of your relationships: D N A

LISTEN: What is God up to? (in my life, or those around me).

LIVE: Where have I seen God at work?

LEARN: What am I learning from my experience over the past week?

This week make sure you address this question:
What practices shall we try this month?

ADDITIONAL NOTES ON THIS PASSAGE:

LOOK: Where in this passage is God calling for my attention?

In the light of this, what might God be saying to me in at least one facet of my life? Circle one, or more, facet of your relationships: D N A

LISTEN: What is God up to? (in my life, or those around me).

LIVE: Where have I seen God at work?

LEARN: What am I learning from my experience over the past week?

This week make sure you address this question:
Who are we praying for?

ADDITIONAL NOTES ON THIS PASSAGE:

LOOK: Where in this passage is God calling for my attention?

In the light of this, what might God be saying to me in at least one facet of my life? Circle one, or more, facet of your relationships: D N A

LISTEN: What is God up to? (in my life, or those around me).

LIVE: Where have I seen God at work?

LEARN: What am I learning from my experience over the past week?

This week make sure you address this question:
How are we getting on with our practices?

ADDITIONAL NOTES ON THIS PASSAGE:

LOOK: Where, primarily over this month, in this passage is God calling for my attention?

In the light of this, what might God be saying to me in at least one facet of my life? Circle one, or more, facet of your relationships: D N A

LISTEN: What, in summary this month, is God up to? (in my life, or those around me).

LIVE: Where, pre-dominantly this month, have I seen God at work?

LEARN: What, mainly, am I learning from my experience over the past month?
Which have you circled most this month (D,N, or A)?

This week make sure you address this question:
How can we encourage one another with our practices?

ADDITIONAL NOTES ON THIS PASSAGE:

AUTHENTICITY - week 1.   MATTHEW 5:1-16.

LOOK: Where in this passage is God calling for my attention?

In the light of this, what might God be saying to me in at least one facet of my life? Circle one, or more, facet of your relationships: D N A

LISTEN: What is God up to? (in my life, or those around me).

LIVE: Where have I seen God at work?

LEARN: What am I learning from my experience over the past week?

This week make sure you address this question:
'Where do I need more momentum?' in relation to 'following' Jesus this month:

ADDITIONAL NOTES ON THIS PASSAGE:

AUTHENTICITY - week 2.   **MATTHEW 5:1-16.**

LOOK: Where in this passage is God calling for my attention?

In the light of this, what might God be saying to me in at least one facet of my life? Circle one, or more, facet of your relationships: D N A

LISTEN: What is God up to? (in my life, or those around me).

LIVE: Where have I seen God at work?

LEARN: What am I learning from my experience over the past week?

This week make sure you address this question:
What practices shall we try this month?

ADDITIONAL NOTES ON THIS PASSAGE:

LOOK: Where in this passage is God calling for my attention?

In the light of this, what might God be saying to me in at least one facet of my life? Circle one, or more, facet of your relationships: D N A

LISTEN: What is God up to? (in my life, or those around me).

LIVE: Where have I seen God at work?

LEARN: What am I learning from my experience over the past week?

This week make sure you address this question:
Who are we praying for?

ADDITIONAL NOTES ON THIS PASSAGE:

AUTHENTICITY - week 4.   MATTHEW 5:1-16.

LOOK: Where in this passage is God calling for my attention?

In the light of this, what might God be saying to me in at least one facet of my life? Circle one, or more, facet of your relationships: D N A

LISTEN: What is God up to? (in my life, or those around me).

LIVE: Where have I seen God at work?

LEARN: What am I learning from my experience over the past week?

This week make sure you address this question:
How are we getting on with our practices?

ADDITIONAL NOTES ON THIS PASSAGE:

AUTHENTICITY – week 5.   **MATTHEW 5:1-16.**

LOOK: Where, primarily over this month, in this passage is God calling for my attention?

In the light of this, what might God be saying to me in at least one facet of my life? Circle one, or more, facet of your relationships: D N A

LISTEN: What, in summary this month, is God up to? (in my life, or those around me).

LIVE: Where, pre-dominantly this month, have I seen God at work?

LEARN: What, mainly, am I learning from my experience over the past month?
Which have you circled most this month (D,N, or A)?

This week make sure you address this question:
How can we encourage one another with our practices?

ADDITIONAL NOTES ON THIS PASSAGE: